EVEN MORE
GAMES TRAINERS PLAY

Other McGraw-Hill Books by John Newstrom and Edward Scannell

Games Trainers Play
More Games Trainers Play
Still More Games Trainers Play

EVEN MORE GAMES TRAINERS PLAY

EXPERIENTIAL LEARNING EXERCISES

Edward E. Scannell

Center for Professional Development and Training

AND

John W. Newstrom

University of Minnesota-Duluth

McGRAW-HILL, INC.

New York   San Francisco   Washington, D.C.   Auckland   Bogotá
Caracas   Lisbon   London   Madrid   Mexico City   Milan
Montreal   New Delhi   San Juan   Singapore
Sydney   Tokyo   Toronto

LOC Number 94-10060

15 16 17   MAL/MAL   09 08

ISBN-13: 978-0-07-046414-8
ISBN-10: 0-07-046414-6

The sponsoring editor for this book was Philip Ruppel, the editing supervisor was Kimberly A. Goff, and the production supervisor was Donald F. Schmidt.

Printed and bound by Malloy Lithographing, Inc.

Like its three predecessors, this book
is dedicated to those countless friends,
colleagues, and co-workers around the
globe who have helped us become better
facilitators--both personally and professionally.

Thank you!

TABLE OF CONTENTS

Publisher's Note:

This book is the fourth in a series of outstandingly successful products compiled by the authors. The first, **Games Trainers Play,** appeared in 1980. Its overwhelming success then stimulated the development of a second book of entirely different "games" which were published in 1983 as **More Games Trainers Play.** This was followed, by popular demand, with **Still More Games Trainers Play,** which appeared in 1991. Now the team of creative authors has, with the input from many other experienced trainers and colleagues, produced a new addition to the series--**Even More Games Trainers Play.** It promises to continue their fine tradition of useful products for trainers, facilitators, and consultants.

Users of the previous three books* have found them to be invaluable aids to a wide variety of training and presentational situations. The books have received high praise from reviewers and users around the world. All four books should be on every trainer's bookshelf--and be well-worn from frequent use!

*The 300+ ideas contained in the first three books have recently been compiled into a single comprehensive reference book, supplemented richly with a broad array of memory aids, trainers' checklists, reference guides, planning and record-keeping forms, and other materials. **The Complete Training Games Kit** is available from McGraw-Hill.

PREFACE

Active learning has become much more than a buzzword in this century. It is a fundamental foundation stone for much that occurs in human resource development. Trainees demand it and organizations must supply it. Training "games"--proven methods of catching and holding trainee interest, or techniques for making critical points powerfully meaningful--have rapidly become essential elements of every trainer's repertoire. Training "games" are proven ways to help trainers, consultants, and facilitators engage the minds of their audiences, hold their attention, and embed key points for long-term retention.

We have been developing, adapting, testing, and refining "games" for trainers for well over two decades. Trainers' demand for them has proven to be nearly insatiable, with well over 100,000 copies of the three earlier "Games Trainers Play" books sold. We have worked hard to bring you a wide variety of all-new ideas in **Even More Games Trainers Play**--each one carefully tested and clearly explained. We are proud of each one.

The format for each "game" uses this standard outline:

> Title
> Objective(s)
> Procedure
> Discussion Questions
> Materials Required
> Approximate Time Needed
> Source

Whenever possible, we have identified the primary source or contributor of the activity. Since many "games" are generic, however, it was not always possible to locate their origin. We apologize if we have overlooked an original source. We greatly appreciate the professionals around the world who have submitted items for possible inclusion. We invite readers with original ideas to complete the "Help Wanted" form at the end of this book and submit your proposal to one of us for consideration. Finally, we wish you great success in the use of **Even More Games Trainers Play** in making your training and presentations even more effective.

Edward E. Scannell
John W. Newstrom

Edward E. Scannell

A member of the National Speakers Association (NSA), Edward E. Scannell has given more than a thousand presentations, seminars, and workshops across the United States and internationally. He was the 1985 recipient of the President's Award from the NSA, and served as the 1987-88 President of the Arizona chapter. He received his C.S.P. (Certified Speaking Professional) designation in 1986. He has served on NSA's Board of Directors, and was the National President for NSA in 1991-92.

Ed has written or co-authored nine books and over fifty articles in the fields of human resource development, communication, creativity, meeting planning, and management. His **Games Trainers Play** series of four books (written with John W. Newstrom) is used by speakers, trainers, facilitators, consultants and meeting planners all around the world.

Actively involved in both civic and professional organizations, he has served on the Boards of Directors of a number of groups including the Tempe Chamber of Commerce, the American Society for Training and Development (ASTD), the National Speakers Association, and Meeting Planners International (MPI). He was the 1982 National President of ASTD and a recipient of its prestigious Gordon M. Bliss award. He later served a two-year term as the Executive Chairman of the Board of the International Federation of Training and Development Organizations. Ed is a Past President of MPI Arizona's Sunbelt Chapter, and its 1986 "Planner of the Year." He was elected MPI International President in 1988-89. He has since served as a trustee for the MPI Educational Research Foundation.

Ed was the Director of the University Conference Bureau at Arizona State University for several years. Prior to that position, he taught at the ASU College of Business and at the University of Northern Iowa. As recognition of his activities, he is listed in:
- "Leaders in Education"
- "Personalities of the West and Midwest"
- "Who's Who in the West"
- "Dictionary of International Biography"
- "Men of Achievement"

Dr. John W. Newstrom

Dr. Newstrom is a university professor, noted author, and consultant to organizations in the areas of training and supervisory development. He is currently a Professor of Human Resource Management in the School of Business and Economics at the University of Minnesota, Duluth, where he teaches courses in Organizational Change, Human Resource Development, and Interpersonal & Group Relations. He has conducted training programs on a wide range of topics for organizations including 3M Co., Lakehead Pipeline, LTV Steel Mining, Blandin Paper Co., Diamond Tool, Minnesota Power, Clyde Iron, City of Scottsdale, Armour-Dial, and St. Luke's Hospital.

John has been active in the American Society for Training and Development (ASTD) since 1971, holding elective offices in the Valley of the Sun (Phoenix) and Lake Superior (Duluth) chapters. His involvement with national ASTD includes a dozen presentations to national conferences, service on the National Board of Directors, Budget and Finance Committee, and as the lead instructor for the "Basics of Training" workshop, which he taught nationally for ASTD for seven years. He was the recipient of a "Special Recognition Award for Outstanding Support to Region VI, ASTD" in 1992. He has been a popular speaker, appearing before many ASTD chapters throughout the United States.

Dr. Newstrom has written ten articles for the **Training and Development Journal** on topics such as needs analysis, evaluation, transfer of training, andragogy, and unlearning; he serves on the Editorial Review Board for the **Journal of Management Development,** and as a reviewer for the **Human Resource Development Quarterly**; and he is the co-author (with Ed Scannell) of the widely-acclaimed books **Games Trainers Play**, **More Games Trainers Play**, and **Still More Games Trainers Play**. He has also co-authored, in recent years, these books:
- **The Manager's Bookshelf** (with Jon Pierce)
- **Organizational Behavior** (with Keith Davis)
- **Windows Into Organizations** (with Jon Pierce)
- **What Every Supervisor Should Know** (with Lester Bittel)
- **Transfer of Training** (with Mary Broad)
- **Leadership and the Leadership Process** (with Jon Pierce)

I.

CLIMATE

SETTING AND

ICEBREAKERS

A RIVER RUNS NEAR IT

OBJECTIVE: To provide an opportunity for strangers to meet and learn where other participants are from; also to encourage initial discussion in small groups and to legitimize interaction & consultation with others.

PROCEDURE: Divide the participants into groups of 4-6 people, and ask them to gather at separate tables.
Inform the group that this is an interactive exercise (with a tight time limit) to enable them to learn more about where other participants come from. Sharing of information is encouraged both within each group and across groups--representatives from each group may "travel" to other group tables to obtain needed information.
Their task is to examine the list of home towns that is provided to them, and place a geographically-correct number on the map that corresponds with the list of home towns for this audience.
Posting of the completed maps allows participants to examine the geographical diversity represented in the overall group.

DISCUSSION QUESTIONS:
1. How many of you could accurately place all the towns on the map? Most of them?
2. What table finished first? Which map has the most accurate placement of town numbers?
3. Who served as leaders (e.g., guiding the discussion, marking the map, going to other tables to collect or share data)?

MATERIALS REQUIRED: Copies of a state map (excluding highways, but showing riverways); marker pen; and a list of all the participants' home towns (numbered from 1-?) for each table.

APPROXIMATE TIME NEEDED: 15 minutes for a group with about 25 towns.

SOURCE: Roxanna Lynn Fredrickson, University of Nebraska Medical Center.

GETTING TO KNOW YOU

OBJECTIVE:	To develop a set of personal reference materials on friends, colleagues, clients, and associates.
PROCEDURE:	Complete one copy of the form that appears page 7 for each key person as a future reference. Make any additional insertions or modifications to the form as you deem necessary. The record-keeping and updating can be done either manually (e.g., hard-copy in a three-ring binder) or stored on a personal computer.
DISCUSSION QUESTIONS:	None.
MATERIALS REQUIRED:	Copies of "Getting to Know You" forms--one for each participant.
APPROXIMATE TIME NEEDED:	2-3 minutes to complete each form (once the data are available).
SOURCE:	Frank Helton, Fountain Hills, Arizona. Also see "The 66-Question Customer Profile" in Harvey Mackay, Swim With the Sharks, (New York: Morrow, 1988), pp. 43-53.

GETTING TO KNOW YOU

Name of Person Interviewed:_____

Job Title:_____

Spouse's Name: _____

Spouse's Employment, or Activities:_____

Children's Names and Ages: _____

Hometown:_____

Person's Hobbies:_____

Spouse's Hobbies: _____

Favorite (or Dream) Vacation:_____

Best Accomplishments:

    Family:_____

    Personal:_____

    Childhood:_____

    Work:_____

Most Memorable Moments:

    Family:_____

    Personal:_____

    Childhood:_____

    Work:_____

Favorite Colors:_____

Favorite Holiday:_____

Favorite Food(s):_____

Strong Feelings Shared:_____

LET ME INTRODUCE YOU

OBJECTIVE: To provide an alternative method to the typical self-introductions at the opening of workshops.

PROCEDURE: After the "Welcome" is given by the facilitator, indicate that you'd like to get to know the other participants in the program. But rather than have each person stand and introduce themselves, distribute to each a 3 x 5 index card. Ask them to print their name, title, and organization on the top of the card. In addition, ask that they identify something about their background, job experience, purpose in attending the seminar, hobbies, hometown, etc. (Dependent on the number of informational items desired, it may be advisable to write out those items on the chalkboard, overhead, or flip chart.)

Collect all the cards and ask a participant at random to pull a card from the deck. As that person's name is read, he/she stands while the information on their card is read to the group. After the introduction, the newly introduced person draws a card from the deck and introduces the person who stands up. Continue through the deck until all are introduced.

COMMENT: Advantages of this method over typical introductions include a lesser pressure on participants, a more casual opening few minutes and a focus on those being introduced rather than the person worrying about what to say. Moreover, it also discourages those "long-winded" folks who just can't wait to tell their own life stories!

DISCUSSION QUESTIONS: None.

MATERIALS REQUIRED: 3 x 5 cards.

APPROXIMATE TIME NEEDED: 15-30 minutes, depending on the number of participants.

SOURCE: Varied.

MEET 'N GREET

OBJECTIVES: To help participants get acquainted, and to help them discover common backgrounds and interests.

PROCEDURE: At the beginning of the workshop, ask people to introduce themselves to as many others as they possibly can in two minutes' time. After those two minutes, tell them to get into groups of three people. Tell them that their assignment for the next two minutes is to find at least three distinctive things that the three of them have in common. The only rule is that the three things cannot be job related (i.e., they work for the same organization). Ask them to identify the three things as quickly as possible and to shout out loudly when they've done so. Provide a token prize for the first team to complete the task. Some examples of areas of commonality could be:
- all are from the same home state
- all have an older brother
- all drive a sports car
- all have degrees in the same field
- all grew up in a single parent home, etc.

After most have completed their assignments, call on a few groups to tell their areas of commonality.

DISCUSSION QUESTIONS:
1. How did some of you complete the task so quickly?
2. Did some of you have difficulty finding common backgrounds or interests?
3. Did anyone discover some startling or surprising information about the others (i.e., all group members are twins)?

MATERIALS REQUIRED: None.

APPROXIMATE TIME NEEDED: 10-15 minutes.

SOURCE: Varied.

NAME THAT TUNE!

OBJECTIVE: To provide a seasonal mixer or climate-setting activity.

PROCEDURE: As a "fun" exercise to be used mainly during the holiday season, this activity can be used for team building, or merely as an enjoyable mixer. Distribute copies of the form provided on page 15 to each participant. Have them form teams of 3 people and see how quickly they are able to finish the task of "Name That Tune".
Award nominal prizes to the team that finishes first.

DISCUSSION QUESTIONS:
1. How difficult was this task? Why?
2. What does this tell us about our capacity to look at old problems in new ways?
3. How valuable was it to work in small groups?
4. Could anyone have done better alone?

MATERIALS REQUIRED: Copies of the form on page 15.

APPROXIMATE TIME NEEDED: 10-15 minutes

SOURCE: Joel Weldon, CPAE, Scottsdale, AZ

NAME THAT TUNE!

Directions: Identify these holiday tunes:

1. Colorless Yuletide _____

2. Castaneous-colored Seed Vesicated in a Conflagration _____
_____

3. Singular Yearning for the Twin Anterior Incisors_____

4. Righteous Darkness_____

5. Arrival Time: 2400 HRS Weather: Cloudless_____

6. Loyal Followers Advance_____

7. Far Off in a Feeder_____

8. Array the Corridors_____

9. Bantam Male Percussionist_____

10. Monarchical Triad_____

11. Nocturnal Noiselessness_____

12. Jehovah Deactivate Blithe Chevaliers_____

13. Red Man En Route to Borough_____

14. Frozen Precipitation Commence_____

15. Proceed and Enlighten on the Pinnacle_____

16. The Quadruped with the Vermillion Proboscis_____

17. Query Regarding Identity of Descendent_____

18. Delight for this Planet _____

19. Give Attention to the Melodious Celestial Beings_____

20. The Dozen Festive 24 Hour Intervals_____

KEY: NAME THAT TUNE!

1. White Christmas
2. Chestnuts Roasting on an Open Fire
3. All I Want for Christmas is My Two Front Teeth
4. Oh Holy Night
5. It Came Upon a Midnight Clear
6. Oh Come All Ye Faithful
7. Away in a Manger
8. Deck the Halls with Boughs of Holly
9. Little Drummer Boy
10. We Three Kings of Orient Are
11. Silent Night
12. God Rest Ye Merry, Gentlemen
13. Santa Claus is Coming to Town
14. Let it Snow...
15. Go Tell it on the Mountain
16. Rudolph the Red Nosed Reindeer
17. What Child is This
18. Joy to the World
19. Hark! The Herald Angels Sing
20. Twelve Days of Christmas

THE GREAT PRETENDER

OBJECTIVE: To be used as an introduction exercise and to explore the validity of first impressions.

PROCEDURE: At the start of the workshop, explain to the participants that they will have a chance to be someone else today. Once they decide who they want to be, they must keep that a secret all day. If participants are already acquainted with some others in the room, they should take seats away from each other. If they decide to just be themselves, that is acceptable, but that, too, must remain a secret.

Once they have decided who they want to be (allow a minute or two for this), break them into subgroups of 3-4 people. At this time, have each person introduce the "person" they are going to be.

For the remainder of the day, participants are to stay in this role. For example, if they are millionaires, they might continually boast of their status, telling stories of their wealth & travels, etc. Toward the end of the seminar, have participants introduce themselves by their real names and state why they chose the character they assumed.

DISCUSSION QUESTIONS:
1. How did it feel being the "Great Pretender"?
2. Were you surprised to learn of others' identities?
3. How do first impressions affect our feelings toward others?
4. How did being someone else make you feel about yourself?

MATERIALS REQUIRED: None

APPROXIMATE TIME NEEDED: 15 minutes at the start of program; 15-20 minutes at the end of the session.

SOURCE: Venus Sage, Ann Arbor, MI

THE HAT PARADE

OBJECTIVE: To provide an unusual icebreaker that encourages participants to focus carefully on at least one part of what might initially appear to be a large course.

PROCEDURE: Develop a collection of hats--the sillier the better. Allocate one hat to each participant as they first enter the training room--either at the registration table, or on their desks.
Ask the trainees to model their hats for each other. (This often produces laughter as they feel silly and look around the room at others feeling silly.) Then ask them to each examine the list of topics and select one that particularly interests them, noting it on a small piece of paper which they then stick on the front of their hats.
Explain that the subject they have chosen will be their "specialist hat" for the day (or course); while they cannot retain everything, they can acquire a detailed knowledge of at least one topic through careful attention and deeper exploration of supplemental materials. Proceed with the course, reminding them periodically through questions like "Whose specialty hat is this topic?" At the end, split them into twos, have them swap hats, and have each "train" the other (a "novice") in their specialty for 10 minutes.

DISCUSSION QUESTIONS:
1. What effect did designation as a "subject-matter expert" have on your attention to that topic?
2. In what ways could cooperative learning like that demonstrated here be used in your job?

MATERIALS REQUIRED:
1. A collection of silly hats, one for each participant. These can often be acquired inexpensively at second-hand shops (or, make cardboard hats).
2. A list of course mini-topics for each student, plus a small card with sticking tape attached to it.

APPROXIMATE TIME NEEDED: 5 minutes at the beginning, 15 minutes at the end.

SOURCE: David Butler, WordPerfect Pacific, Australia.

WHERE AM I FROM?

OBJECTIVE: To be used as an icebreaker and get-acquainted activity.

PROCEDURE: As each person enters the room, affix a stick-on type name tag to his/her back with the name of a state or province on it. They must roam around the room asking questions that can be answered with a "Yes" or "No" response. No open-ended questions are permitted.

The first five individuals that discover their "home" state are awarded a nominal prize.

Alternative: With an international group, you may wish to experiment with countries of the world so that all participants have a fair chance of at least knowing the name and pronunciation of the country to which they have been assigned.

DISCUSSION QUESTIONS:
1. What kinds of questions were most productive?
2. What kinds of questions led nowhere?
3. Did anyone give any clues or hints that helped you?
4. Did you help anyone else?

MATERIALS REQUIRED: Blank name tags (stick-on type) and token prizes.

APPROXIMATE TIME NEEDED: 10 minutes

SOURCE: Unknown

II.

COMMUNICATION

A PICTURE IS WORTH A THOUSAND WORDS

OBJECTIVE: To aid retention for high content workshops and to demonstrate how visuals enhance learning.

PROCEDURE: During the workshop session, create a visual or graphic symbol that represents the key point for that particular module. Show the visual to the group and ensure they understand the rationale and topic that it represents. At the end of the respective module or segment of training (or at morning, lunch, and afternoon breaks), ask the group to individually recap as many of the key points as they can from the segment just completed. Allow 1-2 minutes for this.

NOTE: Most groups will finish quickly! Experience shows that most individuals will recall only about 25-50% of material covered within the past hour or so! Then show the entire group the visual or graphic images that were used during the session. Ask individuals to rewrite the key points represented by these visuals. After two minutes, suggest that participants work in teams of two or three to complete the listing.

DISCUSSION QUESTIONS:
1. How many of you could remember more than half of the key points that were covered? Why, or why not?
2. How effective were the symbols in recapturing your mental notes?
3. Can you suggest additional ways to use this technique?

MATERIALS REQUIRED: None.

APPROXIMATE TIME NEEDED: 8-10 minutes during summary time.

SOURCE: Maggie Bedrosian, Silver Springs, MD; Bob Pike, CSP, Eden Prairie, MN and others.

SAY WHAT?

OBJECTIVE: To illustrate how people sometimes get carried away with their own "impressive" vocabulary.

PROCEDURE: In a session on communication, define the term as "a mutual exchange of information and understanding". In other words, communication is for the purpose of "expressing", not for the purpose of "impressing".
Acknowledge that sometimes we get carried away with our own vocabulary and tend to get a bit esoteric. Particularly in today's society, we see all types of modern, high-tech words and phrases. As a light example of how this can be carried to extremes, pass out copies of the form on page 31. Ask the group to call out any three single numbers, (i.e., "6-1-9"). You quickly respond with the phrase "Optional Management Contingency". Give the group a few minutes to "practice" on their own for other combinations.

DISCUSSION QUESTIONS:
1. Did this exercise make you aware of any of your own excess wording and "impressing" foibles?
2. Do you know anyone that tends to talk like this?
3. What kinds of actions can we take to call attention to others' behaviors in this domain?
4. What are the likely consequences of using language like this?

MATERIALS REQUIRED: Copies of the form on page 31.

APPROXIMATE TIME NEEDED: 5-8 minutes.

SOURCE: Ken Kovach, Cleveland, OH and others.

State of the Art
Systematic Buzz Phrase Synthesizer

Introduction: Anyone who is familiar with the academic, business, or government worlds knows that there seems to be a rule that says "When choosing between a simple and a more abstract (obfuscating!) term, always pick the more confusing one."

In the past, this has been a great setback for clear-headed writers and speakers. But now modern technology has found a solution: the "Systematic Buzz Phrase Synthesizer."

The Synthesizer is simple to use. Whenever you want to say nothing in an authoritative way, simply pick any three-digit number and then find the matching word from each column. For example, 4-2-4 produces "functional monitored programming," which should impress anyone untrained in detecting high-level abstractions. Then you can play games with your colleagues, seeing who can use the most phrases in a day, or who can use such a phrase on a co-worker without getting questioned about it. Have fun!

Column 1	Column 2	Column 3
0 Integrated	0 Management	0 Options
1 Total	1 Organizational	1 Flexibility
2 Systematized	2 Monitored	2 Capability
3 Parallel	3 Reciprocal	3 Mobility
4 Functional	4 Digital	4 Programming
5 Responsive	5 Logistical	5 Concept
6 Optional	6 Transitional	6 Time-phase
7 Synchronized	7 Incremental	7 Projection
8 Compatible	8 Third-generation	8 Hardware
9 Balanced	9 Policy	9 Contingency

TAKE THIS JOB

OBJECTIVE: To develop active and sensory listening skills on controversial topics.

PROCEDURE: Divide the entire group into triads, which will be identified as "A", "B", or "C". Send each group to a different room, or least out of earshot.
Members of Group A are told to think of a topic (controversial & job-related) that all members will talk about when reunited with the other two groups. Groups B and C are given the same instructions. Group A is told privately that they are to play "devil's advocate" to Group B, and also appear to be bored, distracted, or totally uninterested in B's problem. Group A members will do this ONLY to a Group B member.
Have the groups reconvene and form triads, with one member of A, B and C in each subgroup Member B starts speaking first while A listens and C observes and takes notes. When B finishes, A reports back what was heard and C confirms, contradicts, or restates what A supposedly heard. Next, A speaks, B listens, and C observes (paying particular attention to B's behavior). Finally, C speaks and selects A or B to listen and observe.

DISCUSSION QUESTIONS:
1. Ask C's for their reactions andcomments.
2. Ask B's for their own reactions.
3. Ask B's if they felt somewhat 'left out' and why?
4. Inform B's and C's of A's role as devil's advocate. What is their reaction?
5. Have you seen other incidents where people have seemingly quit listening to controversial topics? What were the reasons?

MATERIALS REQUIRED: None.

APPROXIMATE TIME NEEDED: 20-30 minutes.

SOURCE: Linda McCay, Scottsdale, AZ.

THE I'S HAVE IT!

OBJECTIVES: To illustrate how we tend to be more self-centered than we may have thought, and to demonstrate the importance of focusing on the other person.

PROCEDURE: After a discussion on interpersonal skills or any aspect of communication, casually mention that many of us forget about focusing on others and instead become somewhat self-centered, albeit not in a conscious way.

With this in mind, ask the participants to find a partner and for the next two minutes, they will be allowed to talk about anything in the world they want to discuss. There is, however, one rule-they cannot use the word "I". They can do anything else they want; they just can't say "I".

After the two minutes (which is usually interspersed with laughter and high energy), call time out and lead the discussion.

DISCUSSION QUESTIONS:
1. How many of you were able to talk for those two minutes without using the pronoun "I"?
2. Why do so many of us have difficulty avoiding the (over) use of "I" in conversation?
3. How do you feel when talking to (listening to) someone who starts every sentence with "I"?
4. How can we phrase our communications to better focus on the other person?
5. If you did not use the word "I", what strategies did you use to avoid it? Could you do those things more often in your work (or social) environment?

MATERIALS REQUIRED: None.

APPROXIMATE TIME NEEDED: 3-5 minutes.

SOURCE: Sue Hershkowitz, CSP, Scottsdale, AZ.

III.

CONFERENCE

LEADERSHIP

CANDID CAMERA

OBJECTIVES: To help the seminar leader(s) learn the names of participants; to help participants learn each other's names.

PROCEDURE: This may be most valuable, and most viable, for extended workshops (e.g., multi-day, week-long, or those programs that meet in periodical sessions across several weeks).
As participants arrive and register, ask them to pose briefly for a head-and-shoulders photograph. Staple the instantly-developed picture to a biographical sheet for that person, which is then inserted into <u>your</u> own three-ring binder. This is particularly useful for larger-enrollment workshops (over 15) or for trainers who experience difficulty learning names! This allows you to review the bios and photos periodically prior to each session.
<u>Alternative</u>: type up (large print) a roster of all participants in advance of the opening session. Cut the names out, and tape them to a poster board, leaving space for the pictures. As registrants arrive, take their picture and place it in the proper place on the poster. This not only helps you, but provides a "rogue's gallery" that participants can refer to periodically for identifying each other.
<u>Note</u>: Retention of the bio sheets with pictures can be an invaluable tool for refreshing your memory of past participants as the months and years go by. This can also be used in conjunction with the "Who Am I? Who is S/he?" game.

**DISCUSSION
QUESTIONS:** None.

**MATERIALS
REQUIRED:** Instant-developing camera and film.

**APPROXIMATE
TIME NEEDED:** Less than 1 minute per person.

SOURCE: Authors.

DOES A STRAIGHT BEAT A FLUSH?

OBJECTIVE: To stimulate a higher level of member participation in whole-group discussions.

PROCEDURE: Some groups are reluctant to get involved in open discussions, especially if they are first-time trainees, face a complex or threatening issue, or don't feel comfortable with the trainer yet. You can break the ice quickly and stimulate broader (even competitive) group participation in response to your questions by simply following this method:

Inform the group that they will have the opportunity to play one hand of poker at the end of each instructional module (or the end of the day). The person with the best overall poker hand will win some prize. One card will be given to each person every time they make a meaningful contribution to the discussion. Liberally reward participants with randomly-drawn cards as they engage in discussion. Clarify the winning order of poker hands, and identify the best five-card hand in the group.

NOTE: If you deem poker an unacceptable structure for this exercise, simply award the prize to the person with the highest point total (with all face cards counting 10).

DISCUSSION QUESTIONS:
1. What impact did this technique have on your <u>participation</u>?
2. Did this aid or interfere with your <u>learning</u> of the course material?

MATERIALS REQUIRED: Two or more decks of cards, depending on the total number of participants and length of discussion.

APPROXIMATE TIME NEEDED: 5 minutes (to assess the best hands).

SOURCE: The authors.

LET'S PLAY CARDS

OBJECTIVE: To use a creative way of forming small groups.

PROCEDURE: Have each person draw a card from a regular deck of playing cards. If the group is considerably smaller than 52, selectively remove as many cards as necessary to have as many cards as there are participants. If the number exceeds 52, have additional deck(s) ready.

When you want to subdivide the group into smaller subsets, ask for each number cardholder (e.g., those with a "5") to seek each other out and this group will form a team.

NOTE: Depending on the number of participants desired for each discussion period, use various ways to set them up. For example, if you want 10-12 in a group, you can ask that all Diamonds meet in one corner, Hearts in another corner, etc. If you want two very large groups, use red & black. If you want four groups, divide them by suit. If you want to use groups of about 8, you can ask everyone with a "3" or "9" to come forward, etc., If you need a few extra people for a special activity, then designate "deuces wild" and ask them to come forward. There are countless ways to form groups with this method, and the participants enjoy something different than just "counting off by fives."

DISCUSSION QUESTIONS: None.

MATERIALS REQUIRED: Deck(s) of playing cards.

APPROXIMATE TIME NEEDED: Little, if any, additional time is needed.

SOURCE: Unknown

WHO AM I? WHO IS S/HE?

OBJECTIVES: To provide the trainer with a wide variety of information about group members/participants; to provide a format for information sharing among members of an extended seminar, course, or work group.

PROCEDURE: Identify the group members who will be spending significant time together (e.g., one full day or more in a seminar or workshop).
Send a copy of the form on page 47 to all prospective participants in advance, explaining that the information may be shared with their colleagues. Request its return by a specified date prior to the beginning of the training (preferably a week or more in advance).
If possible, reproduce complete sets of the "Who Am I?" sheets and distribute to participants prior to their arrival.
Encourage participants, at the beginning of their time together, to seek out different partners during coffee breaks, lunches, dinners, etc. to explore common interests & probe interesting perspectives.

**DISCUSSION
QUESTIONS:**

1. What did others say that you admired? What comments/items attracted your curiosity?
2. How did others' answers make you reflect on your own? Have you subsequently changed any of your perspectives?

**MATERIALS
REQUIRED:**   Copies of blank "Who Am I?" form for each participant; sets of completed forms for each person.

**APPROXIMATE
TIME NEEDED:**   Virtually none during the training program itself.

SOURCE: Various magazine profiles of famous people.

WHO AM I?

Name: _____ Job Title:_____

Best thing about my job:_____

Worst job I ever had: _____

Most important lesson I've learned:_____

_____

How my friends describe me: _____

How I would describe myself: _____

How I spend my leisure time: _____

_____

My favorite heroes/heroines: _____

If money were no limitation, I'd probably: _____
_____

The achievement I feel proudest of: _____

_____

Favorite advice I give to others: _____

IV.

CREATIVE

PROBLEM

SOLVING

CREATIVE PEOPLE I HAVE KNOWN

OBJECTIVES: To identify traits of creative people and to illustrate the point that these same characteristics are often common to everyone.

PROCEDURE: Ask the group members to think of some friends or colleagues that they consider to be creative people. (In the event that participants seem to have difficulty identifying acquaintances, it is acceptable to list other well-known creative people, i.e., Walt Disney.) Have them write down the names of 4-5 people that fit that category, and then, next to the name of each person, write out what that particular person does that makes him/her creative. These responses could include such things as "always asking questions" or "always willing to take a risk" or "daydreams a lot".
Following this individual activity, form groups of 4-5 participants to compare and contrast the names and qualities of creative people.

DISCUSSION QUESTIONS:

1. As you look over your individual lists, how many of those listed were male? Female? Tall? Short? Older? Younger? (Make the point that physical conditions typically have no correlation with creative abilities.)
2. What are some of the traits or qualities your friends or colleagues exhibit that make them creative? Could you learn these qualities?
3. In your organization, have you seen cases where colleagues show creativity even though the job climate does not seem to foster creativity?
4. How does one become creative in a climate that doesn't currently support creativity?

MATERIALS REQUIRED: None.

APPROXIMATE TIME NEEDED: 10-15 minutes.

SOURCE: Unknown.

CREATIVITY NOT SPOKEN HERE

OBJECTIVE: To uncover several obstacles to creativity that are prevalent in many organizations and to suggest ways of overcoming them.

PROCEDURE: After discussing some elements of creativity (behavioral examples, etc.), acknowledge that in some organizations, creativity is sometimes purposely or inadvertently blocked by policy, people, or the overall culture. Ask the group to form subgroups of 3-4 people and discuss this question: "Why aren't we (or others) as creative as we (they) either could be or should be?"
Give them three minutes to think up as many reasons as they can. Responses will likely include such things as:

Boss	Job climate
No time	Past experience
Lack of skill	Laziness

After 3-4 minutes, ask each group to appoint a spokesperson and identify just a few of their roadblocks. Have a volunteer record these on a flip chart or chalkboard.
After most ideas have been captured, ask each group to go through their own list and identify which of the items listed actually are under their own control as opposed to the control of others.

DISCUSSION QUESTIONS:
1. Were you surprised to see such a long list?
2. Did some of these items hit close to home?
3. For those items listed for which you have some control, how can you overcome those obstacles?
4. For those over which you have no control (Boss, Policy, etc.), how can you lessen these?

MATERIALS REQUIRED: Flip chart, marking pens.

APPROXIMATE TIME NEEDED: 10-15 minutes.

SOURCE: Unknown.

HOW SHARP ARE YOU?

OBJECTIVES: To encourage participants to read carefully, and to search for "hidden wrinkles" that disguise simplistic answers; to stimulate participants to be alert to tiny details and assumptions that hold the key to success.

PROCEDURE: Present the "How Sharp Are You?" quiz to them, allowing a very tight time limit (e.g., 3 minutes). Before you present the correct answers to them, ask them how many had the (most likely) <u>incorrect</u> answer for each one (e.g., 13 hours and 45 minutes for #1; 4 [September, April, June, & November] for #2; 11 for #3). Then present the answers to them, and lead a discussion.

KEY:
1. 1 hour, 45 minutes.
2. 11 months (all but February).
3. 7 pigs lived.
4. 157 (3 x 50, +7).
5. 10 (9 fielders + 1 batter); 13 (9 + 1 batter + 3 baserunners). Add 1 if you count the on-deck batter.
6. "In God We Trust," or "United States Of America."
7. Two hours (now, + 4 half-hours).
8. The match.
9. They aren't playing each other.
10. "Mispelled" is misspelled.

DISCUSSION QUESTIONS:
1. What factors caused you to err?
2. How might those factors affect your work performance?
3. What can you do to control such factors?

MATERIALS REQUIRED: Transparency, or handout of questions.

APPROXIMATE TIME NEEDED: 10-15 minutes.

SOURCE: Unknown.

HOW SHARP ARE YOU?

1. Being very tired, a child went to bed at 7:00 o'clock at night. The child had a morning piano lesson, and therefore set the alarm clock to ring at 8:45. How many hours and minutes of sleep could the child get?_____

2. Some months (like October) have 31 days. Only February has precisely 28 (except in a leap year). How many months have 30 days? _____

3. A farmer had 18 pigs, & all but 7 died. How many were left? _____

4. Divide 50 by 1/3, and add 7. What is the answer? ____

5. What is the minimum number of active baseball players on the playing field during any part of an inning? ____ Maximum? _____

6. What four words appear on every denomination of U.S. currency? _____ _____ _____ _____

7. If a physician gave you five pills and told you to take 1 every half-hour, how long would your supply last?___

8. If you had only one match and entered a cold, dimly-lit room where there was a kerosene lamp, an oil heater, & a wood-burning stove, which would you light 1st?__

9. Two women play checkers. They play five games without a draw game and each woman wins the same number of games. How can this be? _____

10. What word is mispelled in this test? _____

IDEA-SPURRING QUESTIONS

OBJECTIVE: To be used in creativity sessions to encourage more ideas, adaptations, and innovations.

PROCEDURE: After introductory comments on the need for continuing improvement in all segments of any organization, pass out copies of the sheet appearing on page 61. Give the group a couple of minutes to read through the sheet and then call their attention to the first question, "Who". Ask them to provide examples they personally have experienced that illustrate one of these points, or an example they can recall in a general way.
Continue on to the second point, "What" and repeat the discussion, eliciting 4-5 responses of "real-world" examples.
Proceed through the remaining questions, allowing ample time for participant examples.

DISCUSSION QUESTIONS:
1. How can these questions help you in problem solving and innovation?
2. Which set of questions do you find yourself using most often?
3. Which question is the most thought-provoking?
4. What other useful questions have you heard that should be added to the list?

MATERIALS REQUIRED: Copies of the "Idea-Spurring Questions".

APPROXIMATE TIME NEEDED: 10-15 minutes.

SOURCE: Adapted from Alex Osborne's Applied Imagination.

Idea-Spurring Questions

Emerson has stated that "the ability to create is the ability to adapt". Here are some items that can be used as a springboard for other ideas. Change, adapt, add, or delete as necessary.

1. **WHO**
   - Who can help or make contributions?
   - Who must I "sell" on this idea?
   - Who can help me get additional resources?
   - Who will benefit?
   -

2. **WHAT**
   - What do I need by way of additional resources?
   - What techniques or methods can I use?
   - What is the best way? The first step?
   - What will make them "buy"?
   -

3. **WHERE**
   - Where should I start?
   - Where is resistance likely to be found?
   - Where should I "plant seeds?"
   -

4. **WHEN**
   - When should I introduce the plan?
   - When should we implement the ideas?
   - When should we revise our strategy?
   -

5. **WHY**
   - Why should they buy this idea?
   - Why is this way better?
   - Why is the resistance so strong?
   -

6. **HOW**
   - How can we improve on the idea?
   - How can we "test the waters?"
   - How can I persuade centers of influence?
   -

JOE DOODLEBUG

OBJECTIVE: To encourage participants to explore the assumptions they make about problem conditions; to encourage them to learn to ask good questions.

PROCEDURE: Present the "Joe Doodlebug" story to them. Ask them to work either individually or in small groups (leader's preference) to solve the problem. Then lead them in a brief discussion of the exercise.

HINTS:
1. Joe does not necessarily have to face the direction he is jumping.
2. Joe could be at any stage of a series of jumps--he might have jumped 1, 2, or 3 times.

KEY: Joe appears to have just finished the first in a series of four jumps. He is facing north, but is jumping sideways, moving toward the east. Therefore, he must continue to make three more sideways jumps to the east, and then one large sideways jump back to the west to reach the food.

DISCUSSION QUESTIONS:
1. What prevented you from solving the problem?
2. What helped you to "see the light?"
3. What does this exercise tell you about the merits of <u>framing</u> a problem (putting it into a larger context; exploring our assumptions and their implications)?
4. How can we learn to identify extraneous information, and sort it out?
5. How will this exercise help you in the future?

MATERIALS REQUIRED: Copies of the story on page 65 for each participant.

APPROXIMATE TIME NEEDED: 10-15 minutes.

SOURCE: Unknown.

JOE DOODLEBUG STORY

THE SITUATION:

Joe Doodlebug is an imaginary, and somewhat strange, bug. These are his capabilities and limitations in his world:

1. His world is flat.
2. He can only jump (not crawl, fly, walk, roll, or otherwise locomotor across or under the surface of his world).
3. He cannot turn around.
4. He can jump very large distances or very small distances, but not less than one inch per jump nor more than 500 feet per jump.
5. He can jump in only four perfectly-true directions--north, south, east, and west. He cannot jump diagonally (e.g., southeast, northwest).
6. He likes to average 15 feet per jump on a good day.
7. There are no other doodlebugs, or other creatures, to help him.
8. Once he starts in any direction, he must jump four times in that same direction before he can switch to another direction.
9. Joe is totally dependent on his owner to provide his food source.

THE PROBLEM:

Joe has been out jumping all over the place while getting some much-needed exercise. As a matter of fact, Joe has worked up a voracious appetite. Much to his pleasure, his owner appears and places a large pile of delectable food three feet, seven inches directly west of him. Joe wants the food, and he wants it fast. As soon as Joe sees all this wonderful food, he stops dead in his tracks (he is facing north). After all his exercise he is very hungry, and even weak. Therefore, he wants to get to the food as quickly as he possibly can, minimizing especially the number of jumps he makes (it's the starting of a jump--the spring required in his legs--that takes the most energy). After briefly surveying the situation, he realizes that he cannot--at this point--jump due west. Suddenly he exclaims, "I've got it. I'll only have to jump four times to get to the food!"

YOUR TASK:

Accept the fact that Joe was a smart bug, and dead right in his conclusions. Why did Joe Doodlebug have to take precisely four jumps in order to reach the food with a minimum expenditure of energy? Describe the circumstances that Joe must have been in to reach this conclusion.

PIPE DREAMS

OBJECTIVE: To allow participants to practice creativity during a seminar or workshop, and to give themselves "permission" to be creative.

PROCEDURE: Before the session begins, place three pipe cleaners at each person's place. Unless someone asks what they are for, do not tell them their use until mid-morning.
At that time, tell the group that these items are theirs to do--or make--any kind of a personalized sculpture. If asked further, simply restate they can do anything they want to with them. (Urge them to be creative.)
At the end of the morning (or at day's end), ask each table or group of five people to select their winner. Then have the entire group pick out the overall winner.
NOTE: Give special recognition to any group that combines their "resources"(i.e., pipe cleaners), and designs or builds something that uses all their tools. Also, mention that children typically don't wait to ask, they simply go ahead with the task.
Provide small prizes for table winners and the overall champion.

DISCUSSION QUESTIONS:
1. How many were curious this morning (afternoon) when they saw these pipe cleaners?
2. Why didn't you ask their purpose?
3. Why did you wait to be told what to do with them?
4. How many of you opted to approach this task as a team? Who initiated this idea with your group?

MATERIALS REQUIRED: Sufficient pipe cleaners (3 per person).

APPROXIMATE TIME NEEDED: No additional time; interspersed throughout the day.

SOURCE: Peter D. Hopkins, Richmond, BC.

PLEASE PASS THE PROBLEMS

OBJECTIVE: To obtain several possible solutions or suggestions for the participants' current challenges or problems.

PROCEDURE: Ask the participants to form groups of 6-8 people in a circle or around tables. Each person is asked to think about a current job-related problem or concern. Each person writes his/her problem on a blank sheet of paper or on a notepad. Examples might be "How can I get more group-involvement?" or "How can I get my staff to be more punctual?" After allowing a few minutes to think about and write out their problems, ask each person to pass his/her problem to the right. That person reads the problem just received and jots down the first thought(s) that come to mind in addressing that problem. They are given 30 seconds to respond to that individual sheet.
Repeat this process every 30 seconds, and keep the process going until each person gets his/her own sheet back. Time permitting, they can then discuss some of the more practical solutions offered.

DISCUSSION QUESTIONS:
1. Did anyone discover novel solutions that you had not previously considered?
2. Can you see any value in trying some of these suggestions?
3. Do some of these suggestions trigger other ideas or solutions for you?
4. What lesson does this teach us about reaching out to others to their assistance?

MATERIALS REQUIRED: Paper, notepads and pencils.

APPROXIMATE TIME NEEDED: 10-15 minutes.

SOURCE: Susan Brooks, Cookies From Home, Tempe, AZ.

THE PROBLEM-SOLVING WHEEL

OBJECTIVE: To secure possible solutions for participants' questions, concerns or problems.

PROCEDURE: Arrange the room so that chairs can be placed in circular fashion with five chairs encircling five other chairs (double circles). The five persons seated in each chair of the outer rings will be 'consultants' to those in the inner circles who are 'clients'.
The client explains an important question or problem to the consultant for one minute. The consultant has two minutes to discuss, clarify, offer suggestions, etc. After the three minute mark (total), the consultant moves to his/her left and repeats the process with a new 'client' who poses the same question or problem to the new consultant. Repeat this process with the three minute time limit.
Continue for 3 more times and then have the members change to the other circle. (Clients move to the outside circle where they will now be consultants.)
Repeat the entire sequence as time allows.

DISCUSSION QUESTIONS:
1. Did some of you receive some solid, usable answers?
2. Will some of you share your stories?
3. Why is it that many of us have no reservations about telling our problems to total strangers?
4. What kinds of consultant skills were most effective in helping you "open up" and making you receptive to their "solutions"?

MATERIALS REQUIRED: Room with moveable chairs or some setup that allows for rearrangement.

APPROXIMATE TIME NEEDED: 30-45 minutes.

SOURCE: Adapted from Alan Margolis, Hampstead, England.

V.

CUSTOMER

ORIENTATION

HOW FAST IS FAST?

OBJECTIVE: To stimulate participants to think about speed, time, cost, and customer satisfaction.

PROCEDURE: Ask participants these questions regarding the Concorde supersonic jet (answers in parentheses):

1. Approximately <u>when</u> did it begin commercial flights (about 1969)?
   - a. 1960
   - b. 1965
   - c. 1970
   - d. 1975

2. How <u>fast</u> does it fly (about 1350 mph)?
   - a. 1000 mph
   - b. 1300 mph
   - c. 1700 mph
   - d. 2000 mph

3. How many trans-oceanic roundtrip <u>flights</u> was the Concorde designed for (6,700)?
   - a. 7,000
   - b. 14,000
   - c. 21,000
   - d. 28,000

4. What does a roundtrip (New York to London, and return) ticket <u>cost</u> ($2,000)?
   - a. $1,000
   - b. $2,000
   - c. $3,000
   - d. $4,000

DISCUSSION QUESTIONS:

1. How much time is saved by flying the Concorde vs. normal jet planes (about 3 hours each way)?
2. How important is speed to your customers today? How about time? Cost? Satisfaction?

MATERIALS REQUIRED: None.

APPROXIMATE TIME NEEDED: 5-10 minutes.

SOURCE: <u>Frequent Flyer</u>, April 1993, p. 32.

HOW GOOD IS 99.9%?

OBJECTIVE: To make participants think about the impact of mindsets like "that's good enough for me," or "the customer doesn't expect any more than that."

PROCEDURE: Ask participants what quality level, expressed as a percentage of total items produced, they would accept if they were placed in charge of a product line or service. Poll them, by a show of hands, as to the level acceptable to them, e.g.,

Level	# Responses
90?	
95?	
96?	
97?	
98?	
99?	

Then indicate that some contemporary firms have sought to hold their reject rates down to just 1/10th of 1 percent (99.9% quality)! Ask them if they think 99.9% quality is adequate.
Finally, illustrate some of the effects of even a 99.9% quality level by progressively revealing the startling statistics on page 79.
Then you might inform them of Motorola's commitment to achieve "Six Sigma" quality levels-- less than 3 rejects per million items produced!!!

DISCUSSION QUESTIONS:
1. Would _you_ still be satisfied with 99.9% quality?
2. Should our _customers_ be satisfied at that level?

MATERIALS REQUIRED: None.

APPROXIMATE TIME NEEDED: 5-10 minutes.

SOURCE: Joel Barker's book _Future Edge_ and video; Syncrude Canada Ltd.'s _InSight_.

IF 99.9% IS GOOD ENOUGH, THEN . . .

12 newborns will be given to the wrong parents daily.

114,500 mismatched pairs of shoes will be shipped/year.

18,322 pieces of mail will be mishandled/hour.

2,000,000 documents will be lost by the IRS this year.

2.5 million books will be shipped with the wrong covers.

Two planes landing at Chicago's O'Hare airport will be unsafe every day.

315 entries in Webster's dictionary will be misspelled.

20,000 incorrect drug prescriptions will be written this year.

880,000 credit cards in circulation will turn out to have incorrect cardholder information on their magnetic strips.

103,260 income tax returns will be processed incorrectly during the year.

5.5 million cases of soft drinks produced will be flat.

291 pacemaker operations will be performed incorrectly.

3,056 copies of tomorrow's Wall Street Journal will be missing one of the three sections.

KNOW YOUR CUSTOMER

OBJECTIVES: To stimulate participants to use their brains;
to serve as an ice-breaker exercise or warm-up;
to accent the "wealth" that exists in customers
if participants will just look for it.

PROCEDURE: Identify a key word that is relevant to your training
program or central theme of the workshop or
presentation. The example used here to illustrate
the exercise is "Customer."
Indicate to the group that their task, working alone,
is to identify as many legitimate words as they can
from the letters available to them, using each only
once. Ask them to make two predictions--the
number of words they will individually identify, and
the word score of the highest producer. Then give
them a tight time limit (e.g., 5 minutes) and set them
loose on the task.

DISCUSSION QUESTIONS:
1. How many words did you predict you'd find? How
does your own performance expectation compare
to the expectations others held for themselves?
2. Did you exceed your own expectations or fall
short? Why?
3. How many words did you predict could be found?
How does this compare to the actual total?
4. How do you explain the actual results?
5. What does this exercise illustrate to you? (Are
"customers" a rich source of information?)

MATERIALS REQUIRED: None, other than identifying an appropriate word
for the group to analyze. If "customer" is used,
you may wish to create a transparency from the
master word list provided that shows some (but not
all) of the possibilities.

APPROXIMATE TIME NEEDED: 5-10 minutes.

SOURCE: Any number of "WordFind" exercises.

KEY: WHAT'S IN (A) *CUSTOMER?*

Us	Ore	Or
Ort	Use	User
Rest	Rut	Rot
Rote	Rose	Cot
Cost	Cote	Come
Comer	Comes	Course
Cut	Cur	Core
Corset	Court	Sum
Some	Sore	Sot
Sour	Set	To
Tome	Tore	Tomes
To	Me	More
Mouse	Met	Must
Most	Toes	Tour
Custom	Costume	Costumer

VI.

LEARNING AND TRANSFER OF TRAINING

AREN'T GAMES WONDERFUL?

OBJECTIVE: To provide a quick and memorable review of a central workshop theme, while also accenting a small number of relevant supporting questions.

PROCEDURE: Select a key theme for which you'd like the group to have total recall. Create a word game like the example on page 89, with numbered spaces for each letter. Develop a set of clue questions which, if answered correctly, instruct the participants to place certain letters in designated spaces. These should all be stated as "if . . then" clues, and should be derived from the course material.
Distribute a worksheet to each participant, and ask them to work on the assignment individually.
Award a small prize for the first person to finish. Allow a few more minutes for others to complete the exercise, and then ask the early finishers to aid the others by answering the questions.

DISCUSSION QUESTIONS:
1. How many were independently successful?
2. What is the impact of making even a single error?
3. Why is this theme so critically important?

MATERIALS REQUIRED: One pre-selected key phrase from the workshop; a blank worksheet for each participant with the appropriate pattern of numbered spaces, and a set of definitive questions for review (see example).

APPROXIMATE TIME NEEDED: 15 minutes.

SOURCE: Adapted from Rita Johnson, Modern Woodmen of America.

A WORD GAME

$$\overline{1}\ \overline{2}\ \overline{3}\ \overline{4}\ \overline{5}\quad \overline{6}\ \overline{7}\ \overline{8}\quad \overline{9}\ \overline{10}\ \overline{11}\ \overline{12}\ \overline{13}\ \overline{14}\ \overline{15}\ \overline{16}$$

$$\overline{17}\ \overline{18}\ \overline{19}\quad \overline{20}\ \overline{21}\ \overline{22}\ \overline{23}\ \overline{24}\ \overline{25}\ \overline{26}\ \overline{27}\ \overline{28}$$

$$\overline{29}\ \overline{30}\ \overline{31}\ \overline{32}\ \overline{33}!$$

CLUES:

If this day ends in "Y", place an "A" in spaces 2, 11, and 17.

If this book is worth its price, place an "R" in spaces 8, 10, 15, 18, & 25.

If moderate exercise is healthy, place an "O" in spaces 7, 21, 30, & 31.

If "S" is the 19th letter of the alphabet, place it in spaces 5, 16, & 33.

If the U.S. budget deficit is greater than a trillion dollars, place an "N" in spaces 13 & 22.

If 132/4 equals less than 34, place an "M" in space 3 and a "W" in space 20.

If Adlai Stevenson's middle initial was "E," place it in spaces 4, 14, 19, and 24. If not, place a "Z" in those spaces.

If this is a leap year, place a "K" in spaces 6 & 26; if not, place an "F" there.

Think of a popular afternoon non-alcoholic drink in Great Britain. Place the first letter of that drink in spaces 9 and 29.

If George Washington served two presidential terms, place a "P" in spaces 28 and 32; if he served only one, place an "L" in each.

If you are ready to quit this exercise and want a fast finish, place a "D" in space 23, a "U" in space 27, and an "I" in space 12. Can you guess the phrase, even with the letter for space 1 still missing?

EXPECTATIONS FULFILLED!

OBJECTIVE: To glean from participants at the start of any training segment the particular learning expectations they may have for that module.

PROCEDURE: At the beginning of any new topic within a training program, give a blank sheet of paper to each person. Instruct them to write on the page any and all matters or questions that they have about the subject to be discussed. These may be in the form of questions, issues, or concerns they expect to have on that respective segment.

After a few minutes, collect all of the unsigned sheets. Glance through them quickly and summarize some of the more relevant issues or themes, suggesting that these will be addressed. If a few questions are totally outside the scope of that particular phase, thank them for the question and advise them of the situation. TIme permitting, if the area in question is one in which other participants may have expertise or interest, suggest they get together during break times.

Set the papers aside until near the end of that segment. Arbitrarily hand out the sheets to participants in random fashion. Ask them to read the questions on their sheets, and then attempt to respond to the questions. If the question posed is particularly difficult, ask others in the group for assistance.

DISCUSSION QUESTIONS:
1. Did you get your most critical question(s) answered?
2. Did you increase your own ability to answer someone else's questions?

MATERIALS REQUIRED: Blank sheets of paper and pencils.

APPROXIMATE TIME NEEDED: 5 minutes at the start of program; 15 at the close.

SOURCE: Donald W. H. McDonald, Auckland, New Zealand.

FIND-A-WORD REVIEW

OBJECTIVE: To provide participants with a game-oriented device to stimulate their retention of key words & concepts.

PROCEDURE: Select a set of approximately 20 key terms that you wish to accent for review purposes. Fit these into a master 20 x 20 matrix, arranging them in all four directions. Intersect the words whenever feasible, and then complete the matrix with a mixture of other letters that do not spell meaningful words. Prepare a copy of the matrix for each participant.
Instruct the group that their task is to find as many course-related words as they can within the next five minutes, working individually (or in table groups).
When time is up, ask the group to tabulate the number of terms they found in the matrix. Then have members call out all the words they found, so as to help others hear the words one more time. (Alternatively, you may wish to simply display a master list of words, or the matrix with **highlighted** words, to the group.)
Award small prizes to the winning individuals/teams.

DISCUSSION QUESTIONS:

1. Which worked best--blindly looking for meaningful words, or thinking about key words and trying to locate them within the matrix?

2. Why is it difficult for many of us to spot words that appear backwards or spelled from bottom to top?

3. What were the merits of a systematic approach to solving this task, working in all four directions?

MATERIALS REQUIRED: One 20 x 20 matrix, with key words filled in from left to right, right to left, top to bottom, and bottom to top. Then complete the find-a-word matrix by adding miscellaneous letters in all blank spaces.

APPROXIMATE TIME NEEDED: Ten minutes.

SOURCE: Various children's games.

GIVE ME A HAND!

OBJECTIVE: To project participants' future successes by applying concepts learned to real world jobs.

PROCEDURE: Toward the end of the session, tell participants they are about to take an imaginary journey one year hence. Ask them to close their eyes and visualize that they are all right back in this very room for a VIP Awards Banquet. The winners are being recognized for skills and concepts learned and successfully applied over the past year (since attending this program). Each participant will receive the Grand Prize, and their acceptance speech will detail the things they did this last year to win the award.

Ask them to open their eyes and write out 2-3 paragraphs of important elements that they will use in that acceptance speech. Call on several volunteers--as time permits--to hear their speeches. Ask the group to applaud wildly after each of the presentations. If you wish, you may also go to a speciality paper-products store and pick up a supply of inexpensive "Grand Prize" ribbons to distribute to the "winners."

DISCUSSION QUESTIONS:
1. What are the central themes (topics) that received multiple mention in the acceptance speeches?
2. What is the significance of the variety of items that were mentioned?
3. How many of you will commit, right now, to write a letter one year from today indicating your <u>actual</u> use of items from this workshop?

MATERIALS REQUIRED: None.

APPROXIMATE TIME NEEDED: 10-15 minutes.

SOURCE: Adapted from Jerry Gilles, Malibu, CA.

IF YOU WANT MY OPINION . . .

OBJECTIVE: To encourage honest, anonymous feedback from participants for trainer evaluation at the conclusion of a presentation or training program.

PROCEDURE: Place two flip charts at the rear of the training room. On the first, write these words:
"Here are some things we especially valued about this program..."
On the second flip chart, write these words:
"Here are some suggestions as to how this program could be even better..."
Tell participants that you will be leaving the room for the next ten minutes and you sincerely ask their honest evaluation of the program. Ask them to write down their individual responses to the two questions posed. Explain that they should not sign their names, but you would appreciate their specific suggestions and assessment.
Leave the room for at least ten minutes. If participants are still writing their comments after ten minutes, allow a few more minutes. When you return, thank the group for their suggestions and comments.
Tear off the flip charts and return to your office. You may choose to type up the comments and distribute them to relevant audiences (e.g., your boss or the program participants), or you may simply study them yourself to identify any relevant themes or constructive comments affecting things within your control. Then a) celebrate your success, and b) change something needing improvement!

DISCUSSION QUESTIONS: None.

MATERIALS REQUIRED: 2 flip charts and several colored markers.

APPROXIMATE TIME NEEDED: 10-15 minutes.

SOURCE: Christopher P. Davies, Jozsefhegyi, Hungary.

I'M GONNA WRITE MYSELF A LETTER...

OBJECTIVE: To provide a formal method of follow-up and self-contracting for behavior change following a skills-oriented workshop.

PROCEDURE: Toward the closing time of your full day (or longer) workshop, distribute copies of the form on page 101 to each participant. Tell the group that you realize that a lot of material has been covered during the past day or so, and you need their help to facilitate transfer of the training to their jobs. Give them sufficient time to fill out the form, and then distribute blank envelopes which the participants will address to themselves. Have the participants insert the form in their own envelopes, seal them, and pass them in to you. Place postage on the envelope and mail them to the participants about 2-3 weeks after the program.

DISCUSSION QUESTIONS:
1. What impact will writing these contracts have on you and your behavior?
2. How many think that you will be successful in doing the things you told yourself you'd do?
3. What kinds of barriers will make it difficult, or even prevent you from carrying out your promise?

MATERIALS REQUIRED: Forms, envelopes and stamps.

APPROXIMATE TIME NEEDED: 5-10 minutes.

SOURCE: Lou Hampton, Washington, DC; and Mary Broad and John Newstrom, Transfer of Training (Reading: MA: Addison-Wesley), 1992.

MEMORANDUM

TO: _____

FROM: _____

SUBJECT: CONTRACT WITH MYSELF

DATE: _____

The most important or significant ideas that I've learned/thought/
heard/ while at this seminar are_____

_____

_____

As a result of these ideas, I intend to do the following things within the next 30
days:

_____

_____

_____

By doing these things, I will achieve the following results:

_____

_____

NOTE: CHANGE THESE QUESTIONS TO MORE ACCURATELY FIT THE
CONTENT OF THE RESPECTIVE WORKSHOP AS NECESSARY.

IT'S TIME TO SAY GOODBYE

OBJECTIVE: To close a training program of a full day or more in a sharing way by giving/soliciting positive feedback.

PROCEDURE: Use this at the very end of a (multi-day) training program. Announce to the group that, even as this experience is coming to an end, you note there have been many solid friendships built over the last day(s). As the facilitator, you have also gained and learned from them, and you want to give some honest and sincere feedback to them (NOTE: this requires that you have been observant, and probably taken good notes on each participant). You would also appreciate receiving some comments from them (about either you or others) if they feel so inclined.

As an example, you might say to the first person, "Mary, you have given to me and the group your fine sense of humor and have helped make this program a fun one." Or, "Bill, you have given to me and the group a great perspective by sharing your vast experience".

Encourage their feedback to you as well. For example, someone might offer "Sue, you have given me some much-needed encouragement."

NOTE: Although the first few comments to you may come slowly, allow them plenty of time to comment. Once the group sees that you seriously want their feedback, they tend to open up with sincere comments. Allow sufficient time for this before the scheduled closing time.

DISCUSSION QUESTIONS:
1. How many feel comfortable soliciting feedback?
2. How many regularly give out positive feedback?

MATERIALS REQUIRED: None.

APPROXIMATE TIME NEEDED: 15-30 minutes.

SOURCE: Francine Berger, CSP, Stony Brook, NY.

NOW IN THE <u>REAL</u> WORLD WE . . .

OBJECTIVES: To reinforce general principles presented earlier; to provide a foundation for role-playing; and to create mind-maps to aid transfer of training.

PROCEDURE: Form small groups of 3-4 persons per group. Distribute paper & markers to each group. Have them draw a large square, and divide it into four quadrants, which will be four frames of a comic strip called "The Real World." Have each group think of a real work-related situation that could be addressed with material from the training program. Instruct them to create a dialogue between some characters that reflects skills they have already learned. This will require them to draw cartoon characters in four frames (or panels). Tell them <u>not</u> to worry about the quality of their artwork! Ask each group to display their products, and explain what is illustrated (or have the other groups try to figure it out).

DISCUSSION QUESTIONS:
1. What items are now in your skill repertoire?
2. Which ones are potentially most useful?
3. What situations are they most applicable to?
4. What are the barriers to their use?

MATERIALS REQUIRED: One sheet of flip chart paper for each group, plus a set of colored markers.

APPROXIMATE TIME NEEDED: 30 minutes.

SOURCE: Steve Chappell, Chattanooga, Tennessee.

CARTOON ILLUSTRATION

"The Real World"

PLACING THE PROGRAM IN JEOPARDY

OBJECTIVE: To provide a light-hearted, yet competitive, format for reviewing and highlighting key training concepts and terms.

PROCEDURE: Examine the various modules, or key themes, in a workshop program. Divide these into five topics. Develop a set of ten review questions for each topic. Array these in approximate order of difficulty/complexity from lowest to highest. Place the brief answer (1-2 words) for each question into the appropriate column of a 5 x 10 matrix. Cover it up with a piece of stick-on notepaper. Label the columns according to the major themes, and mark the Y (vertical) axis in point increments from top to bottom (e.g., 10, 20, 30, . . .)
Inform the group toward the end of a workshop that they will have the opportunity to play a "Jeopardy"-type game for review purposes. (You may offer a prize to the highest-scoring team. The team with the most points after 30 minutes, or at the end of the game if you want all questions answered, wins.)
Ask a representative of one team to select a category (for 10 points). Uncover the "answer," and allow the first person from either team to raise their hand to attempt to phrase the appropriate question. If it is correct, they receive 10 points (keep a running tally) and the right to select the next category (and next-highest unused point total).

**DISCUSSION
QUESTIONS:**
1. How well did you know the material?
2. What was the impact of public pressure, and of the competition between teams?
3. Will this exercise help you remember key points?

**MATERIALS
REQUIRED:** One poster board, divided into a 5 x 10 matrix.

**APPROXIMATE
TIME NEEDED:** 30-60 minutes.

SOURCE: Rita Johnson, Modern Woodmen of America.

FORMAT: ARE YOU IN JEOPARDY?

POINTS	CATEGORIES				
	A	B	C	D	E
10					
20					
30					
40					
50					
60					
70					
80					
90					
100					

QUICKIE REVIEW

OBJECTIVE: To provide intermediate review checkpoints on retention and learning skills of participants.

PROCEDURE: For full day or longer workshops, this technique is used to measure participant learning in an enjoyable way.

After the morning session, and just prior to the first scheduled break, suggest to the group that a lot of material has already been covered this morning.

To check on what they've learned so far, you're going to do a quick review. Before you break the session for coffee, etc., you need to hear <u>ten things they've learned so far this morning</u>.

Then, as rapidly as possible, ask for responses. After each one, say "Thank you, that's 1" etc., until ten key points are stated.

At the end of the morning session, and just before lunch, repeat the exercise by reminding the group of the content covered and ask for seven things they've learned since the morning break.

Repeat the procedure at mid-afternoon break and again at final closure time.

NOTE: The number of things learned (to be solicited from the group) is arbitrarily chosen each time by the workshop leader.

DISCUSSION QUESTIONS:
1. How many were surprised by the number of items the group was able to generate?
2. What is the value in learning what others considered to be the most important items?
3. In what ways was your list different from that of others?

MATERIALS REQUIRED: None.

APPROXIMATE TIME NEEDED: 2-3 minutes before each break.

SOURCE: Sue Hershkowitz, CSP, Scottsdale, AZ.

THE ALPHABET REVIEW

OBJECTIVE: To encourage participants to stretch their minds and their collective memories, while convincing them that a large number of useful items were learned during a workshop.

PROCEDURE: Form small groups of 3-5 persons. Distribute one copy of the "Alphabet Review" form to each person. Ask the teams to generate at least one significant item (a principle, concept, or conclusion) from the workshop that starts with each letter of the alphabet. Note: be flexible in allowing various adaptations of correctly-spelled words, or "borrowed" adjectives to describe a concept (such as "xcellent customer service"). Then summarize the session by going from group to group and asking for an item that begins with A, then B, then C, etc. Groups will be surprised at the variety of items they identified for different letters.
Alternative: provide the review form and instructions to participants at the beginning of the workshop, thus allowing them to record items as they are introduced to them. This also has the merit of cueing them to watch for at least 26 key items throughout the session.

DISCUSSION QUESTIONS:
1. How much difficulty did you have completing the entire list?
2. How helpful was it to work in small groups? Does this suggest the value of staying in touch with workshop participants at a later date?
3. How many of you were surprised that 26 or more important items could be generated so quickly?

MATERIALS REQUIRED: One copy of the worksheet for each participant.

APPROXIMATE TIME NEEDED: 20-30 minutes.

SOURCE: Adapted from "Body Search" by Creative Training Techniques.

ALPHABET REVIEW

A	B
C	D
E	F
G	H
I	J
K	L
M	N
O	P
Q	R
S	T
U	V
W	X
Y	Z

THE WHEEL OF FORTUNE

OBJECTIVE: To turn a dry review exercise into a game that stimulates closer participant attention and active involvement.

PROCEDURE: Select a short phrase that is appropriately related to either the meeting, participants, or organization. Examples could be "Six-sigma quality" or "Quality is job one" or "Teachers do it with class." Create a blank master on handouts, flip chart, or transparency that shows the appropriate number and spacing of missing letters. Then inform the group that during the review period they will have an opportunity to play "Wheel of Fortune" (without the usual co-hosts seen on TV). Then begin asking a series of answerable review questions, proceeding around the audience in systematic fashion with each successive one. Whenever anyone answers a question correctly, they may guess a letter. If the letter belongs one or more times in the phrase, fill it in and allow that person to try to guess the phrase. When the correct guess is finally given, award a prize to the winner and invite the class to celebrate his/her success with applause. An example is on page 121.

DISCUSSION QUESTION: 1. How did knowing you would be playing a review game help or hinder your retention of key material?

MATERIALS REQUIRED: One relevant phrase, a blank transparency or flip chart with the correct number of blank spaces filled in, and a "prize" for the winner.

APPROXIMATE TIME NEEDED: 10 incremental minutes per game, scattered across a larger block of time spent on review.

SOURCE: Inspired by Bob Pike, Creative Training Techniques.

Clue: "Paths to Survival"

Answer:

_ _ _ _ _ _ _, _ _ _ _ _ _,

_ _ _ _ _ _ _, _ _ _

_ _ _ _ _   _ _ _   _ _ _

_ _ _ _ _ _   _ _

_ _ _ _ _ _ _   _ _ _ _ _ _ _.

Clue: "Paths to Survival"

Answer:

QUALITY, SPEED, SERVICE, AND VALUE ARE THE ROUTES TO FUTURE SUCCESS

TOP TEN REVIEW

OBJECTIVE: To encourage participants to stretch their minds and their collective memories, while convincing them that a large number of useful items were learned during a workshop.

PROCEDURE: Distribute a generous supply of small note cards to each participant at the beginning of a workshop. Ask them to succinctly state one key action principle from the workshop on each card as they think of them. Collect them prior to the final session, and have an aide quickly type them up verbatim on a single master sheet, numbering them 1, 2, 3, 4, etc. Distribute copies to each participant. Then ask them to identify a fixed number of the most meaningful ones (e.g., allow them each to identify, with a check, ten out of a list of 37). Conduct a quick poll of the group (show of hands) for how many chose each one. Count the votes, and inform them of the results for the "Top Ten."
Alternative A: Form small groups of 3-5 persons, and ask each group to arrive at a consensus of the most important action principles.
Alternative B: After collecting the items, end the session but promise them follow-up results within 72 hours. Type up the list of "Top Ten" in order of priority, and mail to the participants as an excellent way to reinforce the key points--as seen through their eyes.

DISCUSSION QUESTIONS:
1. How many items did you generate?
2. How many of your items are on the master list?
3. How helpful was it to work in small groups? What insights did you gain by hearing others' opinions?

MATERIALS REQUIRED: Note cards and one worksheet for each participant.

APPROXIMATE TIME NEEDED: 20-30 minutes.

SOURCE: Unknown.

TOP TEN LIST
(Most Important Action Principles)

1.

2.

3.

4.

5.

6.

7.

8.

9.

10.

WIN, PLACE, SHOW, OR WHAT?

OBJECTIVES: To illustrate the importance of being a top finisher (e.g., 1, 2, or 3); to provide participants with an opportunity to demonstrate the breadth of their knowledge in a light-hearted fashion.

PROCEDURE: Set the stage by illustrating how important it apparently is in society to be competitive. For example, in most athletic events only the first, second, and third-place finishers receive significant recognition. In industry, it is important to be a leader--in product design, in delivery, in service, in cost, in quality, etc. (GE's CEO, Jack Welch, demanded all business segments to be either #1 or #2 in their markets.) In short, we rarely remember the fourth place finishers.
But the fourth item is often critically important. And the mind can capably handle about four substantial items. Demonstrate, by giving the quiz on page 131 (either individually or in small groups). Then let the group score themselves when you solicit the correct answers from them, or provide them to the group.

DISCUSSION QUESTIONS:
1. How do you feel about your memory?
2. Did groups do better than individuals? Why?
3. What are four key things you will never forget about this training program?

MATERIALS REQUIRED: Transparency of the questions, or multiple handouts reproduced.

APPROXIMATE TIME NEEDED: 10-15 minutes.

SOURCE: From the 'Missing Fourth' quiz, by Sydney Harris.

WIN, PLACE, SHOW, OR WHAT?
(The Missing Fourths Quiz)

1. The four largest cities in the world are Mexico City, Tokyo/Yokohama, Sao Paolo, and _____?

2. The "four freedoms" pronounced by President F.D. Roosevelt were Fear, Want, Speech, and _____?

3. The next # in this arithmetic series is 2, 3, 5, & ___?

4. Becoming prime minister in 1940, Winston Churchill told the British people that he could promise to bring them only "blood, toil, tears, and _____?"

5. Area measurements are given in square inches, feet, yards, and _____?

6. The 4-H club members make pledges to Head, Heart, Hands, and _____?

7. The books of the Bible begin with Genesis, Exodus, Leviticus, and _____?

8. The first four presidents of the U.S. were George Washington, John Adams, Thomas Jefferson, and ___?

9. The Greek alphabet begins with the letters alpha, beta, gamma, and _____?

10. The largest lakes in the world are the Caspian Sea (Asia-Europe), Lake Superior (U.S.), Lake Victoria (Africa), and _____?

THE MISSING FOURTHS: Key

1. City--Seoul

2. Freedom--Worship

3. Number--7

4. Churchill's promise--Sweat

5. Area--Rods

6. 4-H pledge--Health

7. Bible book--Numbers

8. President--Madison (or Thomas Jefferson, if you count his second term)

9. Greek letter--Delta

10. Lake--Aral Sea

VII.

MEMORY

CHALLENGES

AND

BRAINTEASERS

BRAINTEASERS
(IQ TESTS)

OBJECTIVE: To introduce any session on creative thinking, problem solving, or any related topic. They can also be used as a "just-for-fun" or change-of-pace activity.

PROCEDURE: Hand out copies of any of the following "IQ" tests (one for each participant). "Walk" them through one or two of the easier items until they get a "feel" for the exercise.

**DISCUSSION
QUESTIONS:**   None.

**MATERIALS
REQUIRED:**   Handout sheet for each participant.

**APPROXIMATE
TIME NEEDED:** 10 minutes for each exercise.

SOURCE: Varied.

I.Q. TEST

Here are some real puzzlers for you! Decipher the
hidden meaning of each set of words.

1	2	3	4
HEAD **LO VE** **HEELS**	**HOM** E	LIP OLIP	Harm
5	6	7	8 **SHAPE**
ROGER	S P L I T	**B A C K** **C K** **K**	
9	10	11 **MUTINY** **CC**	12
NE1410S	**PETS A**		
13	14	15	16
dothepe	TALE	**WORD YYYY**	**LO OSE**

ANSWER SHEET - IQ TEST

1. Head Over Heels In Love
2. Long Letter From Home
3. Tip Toe Through The Tulips
4. Harmonize
5. Roger, Over And Out
6. Split Right Down The Middle
7. Fullback, Half Back, Quarterback
8. Shape Up Or Ship Out
9. Anyone For Tennis?
10. A Step Backwards
11. Mutiny On The High Seas
12. Eye Shadow
13. The Inside Dope
14. Tall Tale
15. Word To The Wise
16. Split Loose

I.Q. TEST

Here are some real puzzlers for you! Decipher the
hidden meaning of each set of words.

1 **1**○	2 **ning**	3 **Fortune**	4 **CI** Life **TY**
5 **L Bus Term L**	6 T K The R C A	7 **I'm nhappy**	8 O DOM
9 **SELF**	10 **LEE**	11 *type*	12 **pre** **+ o** **− ¢**
13 The He He Lurch	14 **O_ER_T_O_**	15 **AG** **E**	16 W G O The Clock N R I K

ANSWER SHEET - IQ TEST

1. Hole In One
2. Lightning
3. Small Fortune
4. Life In The Big City
5. Bus Terminals
6. The Inside Track
7. I'm Unhappy Without You
8. Domino
9. Self-Centered
10. Partially
11. Typewritten
12. Pre-adolescents
13. He's Left Out In The Lurch
14. Painless Operation
15. Agony
16. Working Around The Clock

I.Q. TEST

Here are some real puzzlers for you! Decipher the
hidden meaning of each set of words.

1 **Another 1**	**2** PPOD	**3** CONTRO	**4** BALL
5 **flash**	**6** MORE MORE MORE MORE MORE MORE MORE	**7** OPINION opinion	**8** R Y S
9 The D I A L Hospital	**10** F E E L I N G Dump Dump	**11** Bending ――――― uoy rof	**12** I Right I
13 (N)	**14** MAY AA	**15** w a l k	**16** staying the game

ANSWER SHEET IQ TEST

1. One After Another
2. Pea In The Pod
3. In Complete Control
4. Curve Ball
5. Flashlight
6. Room For One More
7. A Difference Of Opinion
8. Syrup
9. Laid Up In The Hospital
10. Feeling Down In The Dumps
11. Bending Over Backwards For You
12. Right Between The Eyes
13. Encircled
14. Mayonnaise
15. Sidewalks
16. Staying Ahead Of The Game

I.Q. TEST

Here are some real puzzlers for you! Decipher the
hidden meaning of each set of words.

1 role role	2 AMINPM	3 WEL _____ L	4 LOV
5 ERROR ERROR	6 pAI N pAI N	7 Left Out Field	8 1 1 1 1 The 1 1 Block 1 1 1 1
9 Heaven Heaven	10 Die Stranger Die	11 EZ II	12 way yield
13 Are you loneso	14 ISM	15 n n n n n n n a a a a a a a c c c c c c c	16 S S L L O O W W

ANSWER SHEET - IQ TEST

1. Dual Roles
2. In Between Times
3. Well Balanced
4. Endless Love
5. One Mistake On Top Of The Other
6. Growing Pains
7. Out In Left Field
8. Once Around The Block
9. Heavens Above
10. Stranger In Paradise
11. Easy On The Eyes
12. Yield Right Of Way
13. Are You Lonesome Without Me?
14. Capitalism
15. Seven-Up Cans
16. Slows Down

I.Q. TEST

Here are some real puzzlers for you! Decipher the
hidden meaning of each set of words.

---

1 AI 4 D	**2** [EAR] EAR	**3** RIGHT RIGHT	**4** GOL
5 1T3456	**6** abcdefghij	**7** O N A I P	**8** HE AD HE AD
9 BAR Yr Yr BAR Yr Yr Yr Yr Yr Yr Yr Yr	**10** GOOD BETTER	**11** D West D	**12** DR. DR.
13 BENDING DRAW DRAW	**14** 2 3 4 5 6 7 8 9 0	**15** RcAaErG	**16** tion tion

155

ANSWER SHEET - IQ TEST

1. Foreign Aid
2. In One Ear And Out The Other
3. Equal Rights
4. Backlog
5. Tea For Two
6. Typewritten Letters
7. Upright Piano
8. Headquarters
9. Ten Years Behind Bars
10. The Best Is Yet To Come
11. West Indies
12. Paradox
13. Bending Over Backwards
14. No One There
15. Car In Reverse Gear
16. Lotions

I.Q. TEST

Here are some real puzzlers for you! Decipher the
hidden meaning of each set of words.

1 **noon Sunday**	**2** **Kid Kid** (c i n a c i n g vertical)	**3** LB. LB. LB. LB. LB. ————————— **WEIGHT**	**4** CA SE CASE
5 A E I O ‒	**6** **shoot shoot**	**7** QUACK QUACK CLUCK CLUCK	**8** **BRO7**
9 A M Town N	**10** **dknisr** **krinds** **rknids**	**11** X **8** Term	**12** Running Around
13 **Right = Right**	**14** **22** ARIZONA	**15** G W N E I D D	**16** R R R R D O O O O N U U U U U N N N N O D D D D R

159

ANSWER SHEET - IQ TEST

1. Sunday Afternoon
2. Cleaning Up After The Kids
3. Five Pounds Overweight
4. Open And Shut Case
5. Missing You
6. Parachutes
7. Foul Language
8. Half-Brother
9. Man About Town
10. Mixed Drinks
11. Exterminate
12. Running Around In Circles
13. Equal Rights
14. Tucson, Arizona
15. Wedding Ring
16. The Last Roundup

I.Q. TEST

Here are some real puzzlers for you! Decipher the
hidden meaning of each set of words.

1 LA B OR	2 **DEAL**	3 N W E S	4 wolf
5 ¢¢¢¢¢¢ — <u>murder</u>	6 T T A A C C	7 10 10 The Heat 10 10	8 **Decision** **Dec / ision**
9 jury jury jury jury	10 TION TION TION TION TION **GOOD** TION TION TION TION TION	11 **SETTLE** 20 **SETTLE**	12 copy
13 **HOUSE** **STOVE**	14 NOS⅂IW	15 <u>11</u> **TIME**	16 **WAD**

163

ANSWER SHEET - IQ TEST

1. Division Of Labor
2. Shady Deal
3. South Of The Border
4. Lone Wolf
5. Senseless Murder
6. Catsup
7. The Heat Is Intense
8. Split-Second Decision
9. Forgeries
10. Good Intentions
11. A Score To Settle
12. Copyright
13. Home On The Range
14. Flip Wilson
15. Once Upon A Time
16. Tightwad

I.Q. TEST

Here are some real puzzlers for you! Decipher the
hidden meaning of each set of words.

1 **Hard** **x Ahead**	**2** GOOD LAST GOOD LAST	**3** **COW**	**4** Jan. Feb. Mar. DUE
5 over over	**6** π EAR	**7** HANDS HANDS HANDS HANDS HANDS HANDS DECK	**8** PALS CENTURIONS YOKELS
9 Schedule Mon.Tue.Wed.	**10** PIKES PEAK MIDNIGHT ROBERT REDFORD	**11** **worry**	**12** **Me Quit**
13 FINAL FINAL	**14** R R R R U U U U O O O O H H H H	**15** H O W E R	**16** O R N E R Y

ANSWER SHEET - IQ TEST

1. Hard Times Ahead
2. Too Good To Last
3. Holy Cow
4. Three Months Over Due
5. Left-Overs
6. Pioneers
7. All Hands On Deck
8. Friends, Romans, Countrymen
9. Three Days Behind Schedule
10. Tall, Dark, And Handsome
11. Worry Over Nothing
12. Quit Following Me
13. Semi-Finals
14. Hours On End
15. Eisenhower
16. Downright Ornery

I.Q. TEST

Here are some real puzzlers for you! Decipher the
hidden meaning of each set of words.

1 **Sir** **+ Food**	**2** IMPROVEMENT IMPROVEMENT IMPROVEMENT IMPROVEMENT	**3** FA TH	**4** BIRTH 1111 DEATH
5 COF FEE	**6** **IKD**	**7** ENTURY	**8** E L K C U B
9 SKATING i i i i i i	**10** person / ality	**11** $\dfrac{I}{8}$	**12** SCHEDULE Bit
13 A C U M	**14** NAWHAT'SME	**15** D Movie D Movie D Movie	**16** payment

171

ANSWER SHEET - IQ TEST

1. Surplus Food
2. Room For Improvement
3. Blind Faith
4. For Once In A Lifetime
5. Coffee Break
6. Mixed Up Kid
7. Long Time, No See
8. Buckle Up
9. Skating On Thin Ice
10. Split Personality
11. I Overate
12. A Little Bit Behind Schedule
13. See you In The Morning
14. What's In A Name
15. 3-D Movies
16. Low Down Payment

I.Q. TEST

Here are some real puzzlers for you! Decipher the
hidden meaning of each set of words.

1 **Heaven** **— Pennies**	**2** **RAP** **TIMBER**	**3** standing **MISS**	**4** **D E N R U T** **S I D E**
5 **Looking all** **Bargain Bargain** **Bargain Bargain**	**6** **MONEY** **BIRTH**	**7** ♂ ♂ ♀	**8** No No No No **Punch** No No
9 **MAST**	**10** **HOROBOD**	**11** **YGETARTS**	**12** **CC** **TICKET**
13 **JET**	**14** IT IT IT IT **TIME** IT IT IT IT IT IT	**15** **soil**	**16** **Busines**

ANSWER SHEET - IQ TEST

1. Pennies From Heaven
2. Knock On Wood
3. A Big Misunderstanding
4. Turned Upside Down
5. Looking All Over For Bargains
6. Cash On Delivery
7. Odd Man Out
8. Punch In The Nose
9. Half Mast
10. Robin Hood
11. Reverse Strategy
12. Season Ticket
13. Jumbo Jet
14. It's About Time
15. Top Soil
16. Unfinished Business

MANAGERIAL LITERACY: THE ACRONYM TEST

OBJECTIVE: To give participants the opportunity to demonstrate, individually or collectively, their familiarity with common business acronyms.

PROCEDURE: Distribute copies of the "Managerial Literacy" test to each participant (or groups of participants if you wish to demonstrate the benefits of collective effort on a task). Allow them a reasonable, but limited amount of time to work on it. (An alternative is to distribute it at the end of one day of a multi-day course and let them work on it as a social mixer in the evening. A second alternative is to send it to them in advance of the workshop along with other advance readings and pre-work.)

If you wish, they may score themselves by examining the "key" you will display. Then call for a show of hands to identify who got 0-10 correct, 11-20 correct, 21-30 correct, etc. Lead the group in applauding the high-scoring individuals, possibly providing a low-value prize (e.g., candy bar, or drink ticket) to the top scorer.

DISCUSSION QUESTIONS:
1. How pervasive is the use of acronyms as a special language in the business world?
2. What are some of the acronyms that are unique to your organization and industry?
3. What are the dysfunctional aspects of using acronyms in everyday language?

MATERIALS NEEDED: Sufficient copies of the test for each participant; plus a transparency of the "key."

APPROXIMATE TIME NEEDED: 30-45 minutes.

SOURCE: Adapted from Gary Shaw and Jack Weber, <u>Managerial Literacy: What Today's Managers Must Know to Succeed</u>, Homewood, Illinois: Dow Jones-Irwin, 1990.

MANAGERIAL LITERACY TEST

DIRECTIONS: Identify these acronyms:

1.	AFL-CIO	51.	IRS
2.	AI	52.	ISDN
3.	AMEX	53.	IT
4.	AP & AR	54.	JIT
5.	BARS	55.	LAN
6.	BCG matrix	56.	LBO
7.	CAD-CAM	57.	LDC
8.	CAPM	58.	LIFO
9.	CBOE	59.	MBA
10.	CBT	60.	MBO
11.	CD	61.	MBWA
12.	CEO	62.	MIS
13.	CFA	63.	MITI
14.	CFO	64.	MLP
15.	CI	65.	MNC
16.	COGS	66.	MRP
17.	COO	67.	NASDAQS
18.	CPA	68.	NLRA
19.	CPI	69.	NLRB
20.	CPU	70.	NPV
21.	CRP	71.	NYSE
22.	DJIA	72.	OD
23.	DP	73.	OPEC
24.	EBIT	74.	OPIC
25.	ECU	75.	OR
26.	EEC	76.	OSHA
27.	EEOC	77.	OTC
28.	EFT	78.	P&L
29.	EOQ	79.	P,P,&E
30.	EPA	80.	P/E
31.	EPS	81.	PAC
32.	ESOP	82.	PC
33.	FASB	83.	PERT
34.	FAX	84.	PIMS
35.	FDIC	85.	PLC
36.	FICA	86.	PPI
37.	FIFO	87.	PR
38.	FOB	88.	QWL
39.	FSLIC	89.	R&D
40.	FTC	90.	RFP
41.	FY	91.	ROA
42.	GAAP	92.	ROE
43.	GATT	93.	ROI
44.	GDP	94.	S&P
45.	GNP	95.	SBU
46.	HMO	96.	SEC
47.	HRM	97.	SMSA
48.	IMF	98.	TQM
49.	IPO	99.	UAW
50.	IRR	100.	VAT

MANAGERIAL LITERACY TEST: KEY

1. AFL-CIO--American Federation of Labor-Congress of Ind. Organizations
2. AI--Artificial Intelligence
3. AMEX--AMerican (stock) EXchange
4. AP & AR--Accounts Payable and Accounts Receivable
5. BARS--Behaviorally-Anchored Rating Scale
6. BCG matrix--Boston Consulting Group matrix
7. CAD-CAM--Computer-Aided Design/Computer-Aided Manufacturing
8. CAPM--Capital Asset Pricing Model
9. CBOE--Chicago Board Options Exchange
10. CBT--Chicago Board of Trade
11. CD--Certificate of Deposit
12. CEO--Chief Executive Officer
13. CFA--Chartered Financial Analyst
14. CFO--Chief Financial Officer
15. CI--Continuous Improvement
16. COGS--Cost Of Goods Sold
17. COO--Chief Operating Officer
18. CPA--Certified Public Accountant
19. CPI--Consumer Price Index
20. CPU--Central Processing Unit
21. CRP--Capacity Requirements Planning
22. DJIA--Dow Jones Industrial Average
23. DP--Data Processing
24. EBIT--Earnings Before Income Taxes
25. ECU--European Currency Unit
26. EEC--European Economic Community
27. EEOC--Equal Employment Opportunity Commission
28. EFT--Electronic Funds Transfer
29. EOQ--Economic Order Quantity
30. EPA--Environmental Protection Agency
31. EPS--Earnings Per Share
32. ESOP--Employee Stock Ownership Plan
33. FASB--Financial Accounting Standards Board
34. FAX--Facsimile
35. FDIC--Federal Deposit Insurance Corporation
36. FICA--Federal Insurance Contributions Act
37. FIFO--First In, First Out
38. FOB--Free On Board
39. FSLIC--Federal Savings & Loan Insurance Corporation
40. FTC--Federal Trade Commission
41. FY--Fiscal Year
42. GAAP--Generally Accepted Accounting Principles
43. GATT--General Agreement on Tariffs and Trade
44. GDP--Gross Domestic Product
45. GNP--Gross National Product
46. HMO--Health Maintenance Organization
47. HRM--Human Resource Management

48. IMF--International Monetary Fund
49. IPO--Initial Public Offering
50. IRR--Internal Rate of Return
51. IRS--Internal Revenue Service
52. ISDN--Integrated Services Digital Network
53. IT--Information Technology
54. JIT--Just In Time
55. LAN--Local Area Network
56. LBO--Leveraged Buy Out
57. LDC--Less Developed Country
58. LIFO--Last In, First Out
59. MBA--Master of Business Administration
60. MBO--Management By Objectives
61. MBWA--Management By Wandering Around
62. MIS--Management Information Systems
63. MITI--Ministry of International Trade and Industry
64. MLP--Master Limited Partnership
65. MNC--MultiNational Corporation
66. MRP--Materials Requirements Planning
67. NASDAQS--Nat'l. Assoc. of Secur. Dealers Automated Quotation System
68. NLRA--National Labor Relations Act
69. NLRB--National Labor Relations Board
70. NPV--Net Present Value
71. NYSE--New York Stock Exchange
72. OD--Organizational Development
73. OPEC--Organization of Petroleum Exporting Countries
74. OPIC--Overseas Private Investment Corporation
75. OR--Operations Research
76. OSHA--Occupational Safety & Health Act/Administration
77. OTC--Over The Counter
78. P&L--Profit and Loss
79. P,P,&E--Property, Plant, & Equipment
80. P/E--Price/Earnings ratio
81. PAC--Political Action Committee
82. PC--Personal Computer
83. PERT--Program Evaluation & Review Technique
84. PIMS--Profit Impact of Marketing Strategy
85. PLC--Product Life Cycle
86. PPI--Producer Price Index
87. PR--Public Relations
88. QWL--Quality of Work Life
89. R&D--Research & Development
90. RFP--Request For Proposals
91. ROA--Return On Assets
92. ROE--Return On Equity
93. ROI--Return On Investment
94. S&P--Standard & Poor's
95. SBU--Strategic Business Unit
96. SEC--Securities and Exchange Commission
97. SMSA--Standard Metropolitan Statistical Area
98. TQM--Total Quality Management
99. UAW--United Auto Workers
100. VAT--Value Added Tax

MORE ON OXYMORONS

OBJECTIVE: To provide a light-hearted opportunity for individuals or groups to "vent" by sharing some of their accumulated knowledge of incongruous terms or phrases that contain conflicting meanings.

PROCEDURE: This can be used either as a quick break during a concentrated training session, or as a device to draw trainees' attention back to the training session following a refreshment break. It can also be highly effective when it is used almost spontaneously, in response to a trainee's unconscious use of an oxymoronic phrase (e.g., "in my unbiased opinion"). Ask the group to identify oxymorons that they are familiar with, and list these on a flip chart. At the end of the discussion, the following master list of oxymorons can provide a humorous conclusion. "Prizes" can be awarded to those who offer the most creative answers. Alternatively, group competition can be used to see which team generates the largest list in 5 minutes.

DISCUSSION QUESTIONS:
1. Why do oxymorons exist?
2. What is your favorite one (or the most frequently-heard one in this organization)?
3. What role do oxymorons play in the organization?
4. How does this exercise demonstrate the merits of collective effort?

MATERIALS REQUIRED: None, other than a transparency of the master list.

APPROXIMATE TIME NEEDED: 5-10 minutes.

SOURCE: The authors.

OXYMORONS

Acute dullness
Almost perfect
Bad health
Bittersweet
Blameless culprit
Cardinal sin
Clearly confused
Conservative liberal
Constant variable
Deafening silence
Definite maybe
Deliberately thoughtless
Even odds
Exact estimate
Express mail
Extensive briefing
Freezer burn
Friendly takeover
Genuine imitation
Good grief!
Government efficiency
Holy war
Home office
Idiot savant
Instant classic
Intense apathy
Jumbo shrimp
Justifiably paranoid
Larger half
Least favorite
Linear curve
Liquid gas

Mild interest
Military intelligence
Minor miracle
Modern history
Nonalcoholic beer
Nondairy creamer
Normal deviation
Old news
Only choice
Open secret
Original copies
Passively aggressive
Player coach
Pretty ugly
Qualified success
Randomly organized
Real potential
Rock opera
Rolling stop
Same difference
Silent scream
Simply superb
Sweet sorrow
Taped live
Terribly enjoyable
Tragic comedy
Unbiased opinion
Uncrowned king
Unsung hero
Vaguely aware
Wall Street ethics
War games
Working vacation

Source: The New York Public Library Desk Reference, New York: Simon and Schuster, 1989, p. 286.

PLAYING WITH MATCHES

OBJECTIVE: To provide a warm-up exercise, or an opportunity for a change of pace, to a group of participants.

PROCEDURE: Distribute a supply of six match sticks to each member of the total group. Ask each person to arrange the sticks in a configuration such that they create:
- one equilateral triangle
- two equilateral triangles
- three equilateral triangles
- four equilateral triangles
- five equilateral triangles
- six equilateral triangles
- eight equilateral triangles.

Then ask a volunteer to come forward and demonstrate to the entire group the solution to each task. Provide praise or a small reward to each successful person. Lead the group in a discussion of the seminar-related implications of engaging in a task such as this.

DISCUSSION QUESTIONS:
1. Who was able to complete all the figures?
2. What useful guidelines could be shared with participants to help them in this task?
3. What are the impediments to being able to do this task? (What limitations do we place upon ourselves? How can we remove/prevent these?)

MATERIALS REQUIRED: A supply of six matches, or alternative equal-length sticks, for each participant. Also a transparency of the "key" to expedite explanation/illustration to the participants upon completion of the exercise.

APPROXIMATE TIME NEEDED: 10 minutes.

SOURCE: Unknown.

KEY: PLAYING WITH MATCHES

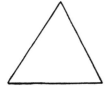

One triangle (with
another one super-
imposed over it.)

2 triangles.

3 triangles

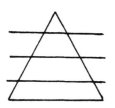

4 triangles.

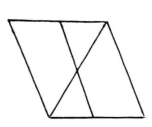

4 triangles
(alternate).

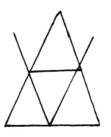

5 triangles.

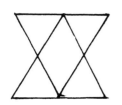

6 triangles.

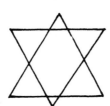

8 triangles.

THE TOP TEN: BEST CITIES FOR BUSINESS

OBJECTIVE: To provide a light-hearted opportunity for individuals or groups to test their knowledge of current business preferences for city locations.

PROCEDURE: This can be used either as a quick break during a concentrated training session, or as a device to draw trainees' attention back to the training session following a refreshment break.
Ask the group to identify the ten best cities for establishing and conducting a business. Answers can be solicited either on an individual basis in open discussion until all ten correct answers appear, or individual "quizzes" can be distributed and unofficially scored by exchanging papers. "Prizes" can be awarded to those who are most successful in generating the answers, either because they have a high total score or because they have come up with the "missing link"--the difficult tenth item. Group competition works particularly well, with a tight time limit. In this way, no one needs to feel embarrassed for not knowing any of the 10 items.

DISCUSSION
QUESTIONS: 1. How did you know the answers?
2. What helps us to retain information such as this?
3. Why might we block data such as this from our permanent brain storage?
4. How does this exercise demonstrate the merits of collective effort?

MATERIALS
REQUIRED: None, other than a transparency of the master list.

APPROXIMATE
TIME NEEDED: 5-10 minutes.

SOURCE: Adapted from annual articles in <u>FORTUNE</u>. Hint: It is wise to update this list annually, as the set of items changes from year to year.

BEST CITIES FOR BUSINESS

1. Salt Lake City

2. Minneapolis/St. Paul

3. Atlanta

4. Sacramento

5. Austin

6. Columbus

7. Dallas/Fort Worth

8. Phoenix

9. Jacksonville

10. Oklahoma City

THE TOP TEN: COMPANY-PAID HOLIDAYS

OBJECTIVE: To provide a light-hearted opportunity for individuals or groups to test their knowledge of current business practice.

PROCEDURE: This can be used either as a quick break during a concentrated training session, or as a device to draw trainees' attention back to the training session following a refreshment break.

Ask the group to identify the ten most widespread company-paid employee holidays. Answers can be solicited either on an individual basis in open discussion until all ten correct answers appear, or individual "quizzes" can be distributed and unofficially scored by exchanging papers. "Prizes" can be awarded to those who are most successful in generating the answers, either because they have a high score or because they have come up with the "missing link"--the difficult tenth item.

Group competition works particularly well, with a tight time limit. In this way, no one needs to feel embarrassed for not knowing any of the 10 items.

DISCUSSION QUESTIONS:
1. How did you know the answers?
2. What helps us to retain information such as this?
3. Why might we block data such as this from our permanent brain storage?
4. How does this exercise demonstrate the merits of collective effort?

MATERIALS REQUIRED: None, other than a transparency of the master list.

APPROXIMATE TIME NEEDED: 5-10 minutes.

SOURCE: Unknown.

COMPANY-PAID HOLIDAYS

1. Christmas Day

2. Labor Day

3. New Year's Day

4. Independence Day

5. Thanksgiving Day

6. Memorial Day

7. Day after Thanksgiving

8. President's Day

9. Day before or after Christmas

10. Good Friday

(Note: Martin Luther King's birthday ranks as the next most-frequent holiday.)

THE TOP TEN: DOWN-SIZERS

OBJECTIVE: To provide a light-hearted opportunity for individuals or groups to demonstrate their awareness of current business knowledge.

PROCEDURE: This can be used either as a quick break during a concentrated training session, or as a device to draw trainees' attention back to the training session following a refreshment break.
Ask the group to identify the ten organizations who have downsized the most during 1992-93. Answers can be solicited either on an individual basis in open discussion until all ten correct answers appear, or individual "quizzes" can be distributed and unofficially scored by exchanging papers. "Prizes" can be awarded to those who are most successful in generating the answers, either because they have a high total score or because they have come up with the "missing link--the difficult tenth item.
Group competition works particularly well, with a tight time limit. In this way, no one feels embarrassed for not knowing any of the 10 items.

DISCUSSION
QUESTIONS:
1. How did you know the answers?
2. What helps us to retain information such as this?
3. Why might we block data such as this from our permanent brain storage?
4. How does this exercise demonstrate the merits of collective effort?

MATERIALS
REQUIRED: None, other than a transparency of the master list.

APPROXIMATE
TIME NEEDED: 5-10 minutes

SOURCE: People Trends, December, 1993, p. 12.

DOWNSIZING:
Largest Staff Reductions Announced*

1. IBM

2. General Motors

3. AT&T

4. U.S. Postal Service

5. Sears

6. Boeing

7. Hughes Aircraft

8. Martin-Marietta

9. DuPont

10. Kodak

*Source: People Trends, December, 1993, p. 12.

THE TOP TEN: U.S. INDUSTRIAL CORPORATIONS

OBJECTIVE: To provide a light-hearted opportunity for individuals or groups to test their knowledge of current business data regarding major corporations.

PROCEDURE: This can be used either as a quick break during a concentrated training session, or as a device to draw trainees' attention back to the training session following a refreshment break.
Ask the group to identify the ten largest United States industrial corporations. Answers can be solicited either on an individual basis in open discussion until all ten correct answers appear, or individual "quizzes" can be distributed and unofficially scored by exchanging papers. "Prizes" can be awarded to those who are most successful in generating the answers, either because they have a high score or because they have come up with the "missing link"--the difficult tenth item.
Group competition works particularly well, with a tight time limit. In this way, no one stands out as drawing a blank on any specific list of 10 items.

DISCUSSION
QUESTIONS: 1. How did you know the answers?
2. What helps us to retain information such as this?
3. Why might we block data such as this from our permanent brain storage?
4. How does this exercise demonstrate the merits of collective effort?

MATERIALS
REQUIRED: None, other than a transparency of the master list.

APPROXIMATE
TIME NEEDED: 5-10 minutes.

SOURCE: Adapted from annual (typically April) articles in FORTUNE. Hint: It is wise to update this list annually, as the set of items changes from year to year.

LARGEST U.S. INDUSTRIAL CORPS.

1. General Motors

2. Ford Motor

3. Exxon

4. IBM

5. General Electric

6. Mobil

7. Philip Morris

8. Chrysler

9. Texaco

10. E.I. Du Pont deNemours

Source: <u>Fortune</u>, 4/18/94, p. 220.

THE TOP TEN: MANAGERIAL TIME-WASTERS

OBJECTIVE: To provide a light-hearted opportunity for individuals or groups to test their knowledge of current business research regarding time-wasters.

PROCEDURE: This can be used either as a quick break during a concentrated training session, or as a device to draw trainees' attention back to the training session following a refreshment break.

Ask the group to identify the ten most significant ways in which a manager's time is wasted.

Answers can be solicited either individually (in open discussion) until all ten correct answers appear, or individual "quizzes" can be distributed and unofficially scored by exchanging papers. "Prizes" can be awarded to those who are most successful in generating the answers, either because they have a high score or because they have come up with the "missing link"--the difficult tenth item.

Group competition works particularly well, with a tight time limit. In this way, no one feels embarrassed for not knowing any of the 10 items.

DISCUSSION QUESTIONS:
1. How did you know the answers?
2. What helps us to retain information such as this?
3. Why might we block data such as this from our permanent brain storage?
4. How does this exercise demonstrate the merits of collective effort?
5. What ideas do you have for using time more effectively?

MATERIALS REQUIRED: None, other than a transparency of the master list.

APPROXIMATE TIME NEEDED: 5-10 minutes.

SOURCE: Unknown.

TIME-WASTERS FOR MANAGERS

1. Crises

2. Telephone calls

3. Poor planning

4. Attempting to do too much

5. Drop-in visitors

6. Poor delegation

7. Personal disorganization

8. Lack of self-discipline

9. Inability to say "no"

10. Procrastination

THE TOP TEN: PARTICIPANT LESSONS

OBJECTIVE: To review key items, or to present important guidelines, to a group in a humorous and familiar fashion.

PROCEDURE: Review the content of a major message or training module. Identify the 10 most important items that <u>you</u> wish the participants to retain. Screen these from least to most important, identifying them as #10, #9, etc.

At the end of a module or session, tell the group that they will now have the opportunity to act as members of the audience at a David Letterman show. In other words, they are about to hear the "Top Ten _____." These could be the most important safety lessons covered, the ten keys to effective communications, or whatever the presentation topic is.

Then progressively reveal the items on the list, going from #10 down through #1. Hint: this will work best if some humor is included, as the example on page 217 shows.

DISCUSSION QUESTIONS:
1. Would anyone like any item clarified?
2. What additional items would you add to the list?
3. Are there any items that should be deleted?

MATERIALS REQUIRED: Previously-prepared transparency, or flip chart showing the ten items in descending order.

APPROXIMATE TIME NEEDED: 5 minutes.

SOURCES: David Letterman TV show; Bob Schondelmeier

THE TOP TEN QUESTIONS TRAINERS ARE ASKED

10. Are we going to finish on time?

9. When is the coffee break?

8. Will there be a vegetarian lunch entree available?

7. Where are the rest rooms?

6. Can I get extra copies of the handouts?

5. Is it OK if I make a few phone calls?

4. Is dinner included in the registration?

3. Shouldn't my boss be attending?

2. How are you qualified to train us?

1. Are you going to cover anything important in the next hour?

THE TOP TEN:
REASONS WHY PEOPLE GET FIRED

OBJECTIVE: To provide a light-hearted opportunity for individuals or groups to test their knowledge of current business facts.

PROCEDURE: This can be used either as a quick break during a concentrated training session, or as a device to draw trainees' attention back to the training session following a refreshment break.

Ask the group to identify the ten most important reasons why people get fired from work. Answers can be solicited either on an individual basis in open discussion until all ten correct answers appear, or individual "quizzes" can be distributed and unofficially scored by exchanging papers. "Prizes" can be awarded to those who are most successful in generating the answers, either because they have a high score or because they have come up with the "missing link"--the difficult tenth item.

Group competition works particularly well, with a tight time limit. In this way, no one feels embarrassed for not knowing any of the 10 items.

DISCUSSION QUESTIONS:
1. How did you know the answers?
2. What helps us to retain information such as this?
3. Why might we block data such as this from our permanent brain storage?
4. How does this exercise demonstrate the merits of collective effort?

MATERIALS REQUIRED: None, other than a transparency of the master list.

APPROXIMATE TIME NEEDED: 5-10 minutes.

SOURCE: Marilyn Moats Kennedy, Business Week Careers, no date, pp. 39-41.

REASONS FOR FIRING

1. Poor fit with the corporate culture.

2. Over-selling one's qualifications.

3. Bad chemistry with the boss.

4. Rigidity (clinging to old experiences).

5. Lack of necessary job skills.

6. Victim of a power play.

7. Refusal to conform to unspoken rules.

8. Failing to be a team player.

9. Business cutbacks (plus mergers).

10. Poor judgment.

Source: M.M. Kennedy, <u>Business Week Careers</u>, n.d., pp. 39-41.

THE TOP TEN: RELOCATION REASONS

OBJECTIVE: To provide a light-hearted opportunity for individuals or groups to test their knowledge of current business phenomena.

PROCEDURE: This can be used either as a quick break during a concentrated training session, or as a device to draw trainees' attention back to the training session following a refreshment break.
Ask the group to identify the ten most important reasons for relocating a business. Answers can be solicited either on an individual basis in open discussion until all ten correct answers appear, or individual "quizzes" can be distributed and unofficially scored by exchanging papers. "Prizes" can be awarded to those who are most successful in generating the answers, either because they have a high score or because they have come up with the "missing link"--the difficult tenth item.
Group competition works particularly well, with a tight time limit. In this way, no one feels embarrassed for not knowing any of the 10 items.

DISCUSSION QUESTIONS:
1. How did you know the answers?
2. What helps us to retain information such as this?
3. Why might we block data such as this from our permanent brain storage?
4. How does this exercise demonstrate the merits of collective effort?

MATERIALS REQUIRED: None, other than a transparency of the master list.

APPROXIMATE TIME NEEDED: 5-10 minutes.

SOURCE: Unknown.

CORPORATE RELOCATION REASONS

1. High local labor costs.

2. High operating costs (taxes; utilities).

3. Shortage of productive employees.

4. Recruiting problems (attracting).

5. Union pressures and problems.

6. High state taxes.

7. Long commutes.

8. Declining lifestyles.

9. High crime rate.

10. CEO/owner wants to move.

THE TOP TEN: SMALL BUSINESS CONCERNS

OBJECTIVE: To provide a light-hearted opportunity for individuals or groups to test their knowledge of current business concerns.

PROCEDURE: This can be used either as a quick break during a concentrated training session, or as a device to draw trainees' attention back to the training session following a refreshment break.
Ask the group to identify the ten most significant concerns of small business owners. Answers can be solicited either on an individual basis in open discussion until all ten correct answers appear, or individual "quizzes" can be distributed and unofficially scored by exchanging papers. "Prizes" can be awarded to those who are most successful in generating the answers, either because they have a high score or because they have come up with the "missing link"--the difficult tenth item.
Group competition works particularly well, with a tight time limit. In this way, no one feels embarrassed for not knowing any of the 10 items.

DISCUSSION QUESTIONS:
1. How did you know the answers?
2. What helps us to retain information such as this?
3. Why might we block data such as this from our permanent brain storage?
4. How does this exercise demonstrate the merits of collective effort?

MATERIALS REQUIRED: None, other than a transparency of the master list.

APPROXIMATE TIME NEEDED: 5-10 minutes.

SOURCE: NATION'S BUSINESS, February, 1991, p. 45.

SMALL BUSINESS OWNERS: THEIR TOP CONCERNS

1. Cost of health care.

2. Cost of employee benefits.

3. Impact of the local economy.

4. Cost of property insurance.

5. Pricing pressures.

6. Regulatory compliance costs.

7. Cash flow.

8. Balancing quality and costs.

9. Credit crunch limiting their growth.

10. Low worker productivity.

Source: <u>Nation's Business</u>, 2/91, p. 45.

VIII.

PARADIGM-

BREAKING

AND

CHANGE

CHANGE THE PICTURE & THE PARADIGM

OBJECTIVE: To encourage participants to move flexibly from one paradigm (framework, or mind set) to another.

PROCEDURE: Provide the group with a large set of pictures or colored advertisements. Let each individual choose their own materials (one picture).
Ask them to cut their picture into small pieces such that they lose their original identity (and simply become new, smaller, colored shapes).
Now instruct them to assemble the pieces into a collage of their own design, and create a title for it. Have each participant show their collage to their group, and also explain what it was before it underwent a transformation.

ALTERNATIVE PROCEDURE: Give them a focused assignment consistent with the workshop's theme, such as "Change" or "Service" or "Quality" or "Speed."

DISCUSSION QUESTIONS:
1. How did it feel to convert one image to another?
2. How difficult was it to "let go" of the original?
3. What is involved in casting aside older paradigms and creating or adopting new ones?
4. What examples can you provide of people or organizations that have successfully replaced their paradigms?

MATERIALS REQUIRED: Old magazines or magazine advertisements, plus some flip chart paper for a base, scissors, and glue or rubber cement for each person.

APPROXIMATE TIME NEEDED: 30-45 minutes.

SOURCE: Unknown.

DON'T PUSH ME!

OBJECTIVE: To illustrate the importance of passive resistance.

PROCEDURE: This exercise is particularly appropriate when participants need a quick break during long sessions. It allows them to stand and move around a bit, but keeps them centered on the material. Ask participants to stand and pair off, facing their partner about three feet away. Designate one person in each dyad as "A" and the other as "B". Each person places his/her hands against the hands of the partner. Hands should be at shoulder height with palms open and forward.

Tell attendees to press their hands against their partners with firm and equal pressure. Ask partner "A" to remove hands quickly--and without warning--any time in the next few moments.

After all "A" partners have done so, repeat the process, but with partner "B" pulling back at their discretion.

DISCUSSION QUESTIONS:
1. What was your reaction when your partner pulled away?
2. What was your feeling when you no longer felt any resistance?
3. How many of you seemed to "fall" into your partner's space when they stopped resisting?
4. Have you observed situations when people have actually "gained" by removing some of the "pressures" we place on others? Please describe.
5. Under what conditions should we "push," and when should we learn to "give in"?

MATERIALS REQUIRED: None.

APPROXIMATE TIME NEEDED: 5 minutes.

SOURCE: Carol Klein-Zemp, Phoenix, AZ.

LET'S GET MOVING!

OBJECTIVE: To engage participants in a practice exercise for enacting a change using the "force-field" technique.

PROCEDURE: Distribute copies of the "Action Plan" to each participant. Explain that this tool called "force-field analysis" was first used by Kurt Lewin. Walk them through the form so they can use it later.
1. Fill in the organization's name.
2. Goals: These are often stated in general terms. Have them write out 2-3 overall goals.
3. Objectives: Specify what they want to change or accomplish. For example, "Reduce absenteeism by 10% in the next ten weeks."
4. Driving Forces: List those items that are "pushing" the change or action, i.e., "The boss says so."
5. Restraining Forces: Write out those factors that tend to hold back or block the change from taking place, i.e., "Not enough resources", etc. Suggest to the group that for change to be successfully made, each restraining force must be removed or lessened. Have the group suggest ways of doing so for the items listed.
6. Timetable: Actually write out some interim dates and commit to those actions being done.
7. Commitment: State exactly what priority and how committed you are to seeing this change or action through to its completion.

DISCUSSION QUESTIONS:
1. In what ways can this tool be useful to you?
2. What are its shortcomings?
3. What suggestions can you make for revising or adapting it?

MATERIALS REQUIRED: Copies of "Action Plan."

APPROXIMATE TIME NEEDED: 20-30 minutes.

SOURCE: Unknown.

ACTION PLAN

1. ORGANIZATION _____

2. GOALS (What do you want to do? What is the purpose?):
   _____
   _____

3. OBJECTIVES (Some specific targets):

   A. _____
   B. _____
   C. _____
   D. _____

4. DRIVING FORCES:

   A. _____
   B. _____
   C. _____
   D. _____

5. RESTRAINING FORCES:

   A. _____
   B. _____
   C. _____
   D. _____

6. TIMETABLE:

   <u>Date</u>   <u>Action</u>
   A. _____   _____
   B. _____   _____
   C. _____   _____
   D. _____   _____

7. COMMITMENT:

   _____
   _____
   _____

MANAGING CHANGE

OBJECTIVES: To provide participants with an opportunity to analyze the change process and decide how to make future changes more readily acceptable.

PROCEDURE: Divide the group into subgroups of 4-5 participants, preferably from different organizations or divisions. Then ask them to discuss the following questions with their group members:
1. Identify a recent situation in which some type of change was introduced in your organization (division, agency, etc.). Provide a brief synopsis of that change and how it was initiated.
2. Was the change resisted?
3. Why or why not?
4. In retrospect, what would (should) have been done to make the change easier?

NOTE: Allow 10-15 minutes for group discussion. After groups have finished their assignments, call on random spokespersons to report on their discussions, spending most of their oral report on question #4 (i.e., "if we (they) had known then what we (they) know now, what should have been done to make that change easier?"

Responses will usually center around such items as "better planning", "communication", "no surprises", etc.

DISCUSSION QUESTIONS:
1. What was done to add to the forces strengthening the proposed change?
2. What was done to weaken or remove the forces resisting the change?
3. At what stage did the tide turn in favor (or against!) the proposed change? Why?

MATERIALS REQUIRED: None.

APPROXIMATE TIME NEEDED: 20-30 minutes.

SOURCE: Unknown.

242

THE 10 PERCENT STRETCH

OBJECTIVE: To impress upon audience members that no matter how well they are performing now, they are probably capable of doing better.

PROCEDURE: Ask a volunteer to step to the side of the room. Request that the person extend an arm and reach as high on the wall as s/he can. Be prepared to have some way to assess approximately how high the person's outstretched fingertips reached. Now ask them to extend their arm again and, by really stretching themselves, reach as high on the wall as they can. Note how far their fingertips extended this time (it will invariably be further). Stress a few major points from this exercise (or, preferably, ask the group to derive its own conclusions from the demonstration). Ask them to note the effects of a 10% improvement by a baseball player, for example--more hits, more total bases, fewer errors.

DISCUSSION QUESTIONS:
1. What apprehensions do we have about doing something new or different?
2. Could you improve your performance in some area by 10% or more? In what areas?
3. What message might you be sending to workers when you emphasize the value of a 10% improvement in performance at work?
4. In what ways have we "learned" to hold some portion of our energy/talent in reserve?

MATERIALS REQUIRED: None.

APPROXIMATE TIME NEEDED: 5-10 minutes, depending on discussion time.

SOURCE: Richard L. Hughes, et. al., Leadership, (Homewood, Illinois: Irwin), 1993, pp. 37-39.

WHO ARE THESE PEOPLE?

OBJECTIVE: To stimulate participants to look for new patterns and paradigms, by breaking out of old ways of seeing things.

PROCEDURE: Show participants the ten anagrams on page 247. Give them several minutes to solve them by rearranging the letters to identify a common profession for each.

KEY:
1. TRAINERS
2. DOCTORS
3. CUSTODIAN
4. WAITRESS
5. GOLFER
6. MANAGERS
7. TEACHER
8. AUTHORS
9. LAWYERS
10. ARTIST

NOTE: For variety in another session (after they are done with this exercise) ask them to create a new set of anagrams for ten other professions, or for ten of the company's products or locations.

DISCUSSION QUESTIONS:
1. What prevented you from seeing the answers?
2. What helped you solve the anagrams?
3. What paradigms do you hold that serve as restrictions or constraints?

MATERIALS REQUIRED: Transparency of the anagrams.

APPROXIMATE TIME NEEDED: 15 minutes.

SOURCE: Eve Wirth, The Riddle Box.

246

WHO ARE THESE PEOPLE?
(Rearrange the letters to identify a common profession)

Clue	Profession
1. IN ARREST	1. _____
2. COD ROTS	2. _____
3. A COIN STUD	3. _____
4. STEW A SIR	4. _____
5. LOG REF	5. _____
6. SNAG MARE	6. _____
7. CHEATER	7. _____
8. SOUR HAT	8. _____
9. SLY WARE	9. _____
10. IS TART	10. _____

ZIP UP YOUR ZIP CODES; DIAL YOUR PHONE

OBJECTIVE: To stimulate participants to examine their assumptions about a common phenomenon, explore the implications of unused potential in organizations and individuals, and increase our observational skills.

PROCEDURE: Ask trainees to write down four items on a sheet of paper:

1. The lowest zip code in the United States.
2. The highest zip code in the United States.
3. The two letters of the alphabet that are NOT used on current touch-tone phones.
4. The non numeric, non alphabetical symbols that appear on a 12-key phone.

Then ask them to score themselves according to the following key:

1. Lowest zip: 00401 (held by the Readers Digest Association in Pleasantville, NY.)
2. Highest zip: 99950 (Ketchikan, Alaska)
3. Missing letters: Q & Z
4. Symbols: "*" and "#"

DISCUSSION QUESTIONS:

1. What does the range of zip codes teach us about unused potential in our organizations? Is this indicative of the unused potential in individuals?
2. What assumptions (paradigms) led us to judge incorrectly the highest and lowest zip codes?
3. Why do we overlook "obvious" things that are visible to us on a daily basis?

MATERIALS REQUIRED: None.

APPROXIMATE TIME NEEDED: 5-10 minutes.

SOURCE: Adapted from information in "Fixit," <u>Minneapolis Star Tribune</u>, n.d., Minneapolis, MN 55488.

IX.

PRESENTATION

TOOLS

BEGINNINGS AND ENDINGS

OBJECTIVE: To demonstrate that sometimes two or more different things actually have no clear distinction between their boundaries; the ending of one may become the beginning of another.

PROCEDURE: Take a strip of soft paper that is narrow and long (e.g., 4" x 20"). Lay it on a table before a group. Ask them if anyone can demonstrate how they can take a pencil and start drawing a line down the length of the paper, and, <u>without ever releasing the pressure on the paper</u> (and the table) continue that same line across the entire length of the <u>other side</u> of the paper strip.

If (when) no one can do it, demonstrate how it can be done by converting the paper into a Mobius strip. (See the illustration on page 255.) Ask a volunteer to come forward and begin drawing the line. As they get half-way across the strip, pick up the initial end, give it a one-half twist, and connect it to the remaining end. Allow them to progress by laying down more of the strip (and pulling up the used section). Their path will come full circle.

DISCUSSION QUESTION:

1. What kinds of things do we encounter that seem to be totally separate and distinct, yet actually blend together? (An example is one person's responsibility for a certain phase of a project, and another's beginning of the next phase. Where does one begin and the other end?)
2. What kinds of things do we encounter that seem to blend together, yet actually are separate and distinct?

MATERIALS REQUIRED: One long strip of paper, tape, and a pencil.

APPROXIMATE TIME NEEDED: 5 minutes.

SOURCE: Any book addressing topographical mathematics.

THE MOBIUS STRIP

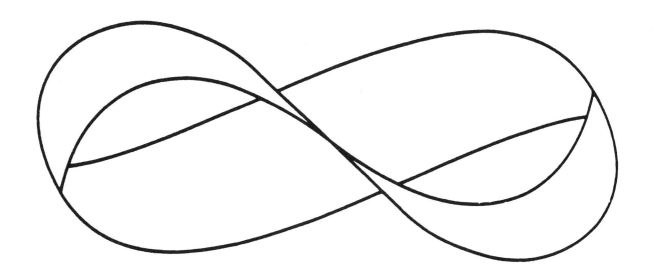

GLAD TO MEET YOU -- SORT OF

OBJECTIVE: To illustrate the importance of first impressions and to show how body language can contradict or reinforce verbal messages.

PROCEDURE: Ask the group to form subgroups of 5 people. They will be asked to "meet and greet" each other in each of the following ways:
- They really don't want to meet the other person.
- They fear the other may reject their greeting.
- They already know they are friends.
- They already know the person--but just a little bit.

After each of the above four role-plays are announced, allow 3-4 minutes for each activity so everyone can experience the activity. Then direct them to rotate to a new person and conduct the next role play.

DISCUSSION QUESTIONS:
1. How did you feel the first time when you weren't really overly thrilled (to put it mildly) to be meeting the other person?
2. What influences you most when making first contact?
3. Did your nonverbal behavior reinforce or negate your words or feelings?
4. Why were the first two activities uncomfortable?
5. Can your nonverbal cues speak more "loudly" than your words? Are you conscious of your range of nonverbal signals?

MATERIALS REQUIRED: None.

APPROXIMATE TIME NEEDED: 12-15 minutes.

SOURCE: Adapted from Tony Robbins, San Diego, CA.

K.I.S.S.: KEEP IT SIMPLE, SILLY

OBJECTIVE: To provide a demonstration of the merits of finding and using simple ways to present information to others to expedite learning and retention.

PROCEDURE: Divide the participants into three groups. Give each group a different set of materials, as follows:
1. A set of seven phrases that describe the "seven deadly sins" in rich detail (with those words blended into the list).
2. A set of seven words that list, in order, the "seven deadly sins."
3. A set of seven words (with a nonsense acronym--PAWSLEG--to cue them).

Give all participants exactly 30 seconds to learn the material. Then ask each group to set aside the document given them, and write the seven deadly sins <u>in order</u> on a separate sheet of paper (in one minute). Display the list of the sins, and ask them to score themselves. Compute an average score for each group.

DISCUSSION QUESTIONS:
1. Which group did the best? Why?
2. What are some ways in which you could use acronyms in your job to help you remember?
3. What are the risks of teaching/learning through the use of acronyms?
4. In what ways can the "KISS principle" be applied to your job?

MATERIALS REQUIRED: None, other than a transparency of the master list.

APPROXIMATE TIME NEEDED: 5-10 minutes.

SOURCE: The authors.

THE "SEVEN DEADLY SINS"

1. Pride, conceit, over-indulged self-esteem

2. Avarice, greed

3. Wrath, violent anger, rage, fury

4. Sloth, laziness, indolence

5. Lust, intense and obsessive desire

6. Envy and shameful desire for another's possessions

7. Gluttony and immoderate consumption

THE "SEVEN DEADLY SINS"

1. Pride

2. Avarice

3. Wrath

4. Sloth

5. Lust

6. Envy

7. Gluttony

THE "SEVEN DEADLY SINS"

Pride

Avarice

Wrath

Sloth

Lust

Envy

Gluttony

(Note the memory-jogging acronym created by using the first letter of each word: **PAWSLEG**.)

MUSICAL AUDIENCES

OBJECTIVE: To allow participants practice in altering their own presentations for different audiences.

PROCEDURE: Divide the group into subgroups of five and ask them to arrange their chairs in a small circle. The person whose birthday is closest to today is designated the first "speaker". Hold up the first "Audience ID Card" (for example, "engineers") and tell the group they are now all engineers and should expect to be addressed as such. Whenever they hear the bell, they are to look for their new identities, and assume those roles. The speaker, of course, will be expected to adjust the presentation accordingly.
When everyone is ready to begin, hold up the first "Speaker's Topic" card and tell them to begin immediately. Once the process begins, ring the bell every 2-3 minutes to change "Audience ID" card and begin.
Continue the process for the rest of the "speakers" as time permits.

DISCUSSION QUESTIONS:
1. How difficult was it to adjust to your new audience?
2. How uncomfortable was it to start speaking with no preparation time?
3. What were some of the techniques you used to adapt?
4. Have you observed speakers or trainers who seemingly give the exact same talk regardless of their audiences?

MATERIALS REQUIRED: "Speaker ID" and "Audience ID" cards and a bell.

APPROXIMATE TIME NEEDED: 20-40 minutes.

SOURCE: Ellen Dowling, Ph.D., Corrales, NM.

Musical Audience ID Cards

Possible audience cards:
- Accountants
- Astronauts
- Artists
- Auctioneers
- Bankers
- Booksellers
- Biologists
- Computer sales personnel
- Coaches
- Custodians
- Democrats
    etc.

Suggested topics:
- Applications of leadership
- Book reviews
- Communication skills
- Diversity training
- Employee attitudes
- Future trends
- Globalization
    etc.

SOMETHING IN THE AIR

OBJECTIVE: To demonstrate the powers of positive and negative energies within a group.

PROCEDURE: Tell the group that you are about to vividly demonstrate the power within the room. We often talk about group "energy;" we are about to show it! Ask for a male and a female volunteer to come to the front of the room. Assure them that no one will be embarrassed and that it is a demonstration to show the effects of positive and negative energy. As the man faces the audience, ask him to raise his right arm to be parallel with the floor. Ask the woman to stand behind the man and place two fingers of her right hand on his right wrist. Ask her then to try and push his arm down as he resists. (Likely, she will not be able to.) Ask the group to "send" the man some positive energy, i.e., smiles, warm thoughts, applause, etc. Then ask the woman to again push his wrist downward while he resists. Doubtless, she will again be unsuccessful.
Now, tell the group to "send" some negative vibes or energy (frowns, negative thoughts, etc.) toward the man. Ask the woman to try one more time to push down. In all likelihood, she can now do so easily!

DISCUSSION QUESTIONS:
1. Ask the male if he resisted equally all three times. Ask the woman if she used the same pressure each time.
2. Ask the male if he "felt" differently when either the positive or negative energies were sent to him.
3. Ask the audience if they've experienced "feeling" such positive or negative strokes.

MATERIALS REQUIRED: None.

APPROXIMATE TIME NEEDED: 5 minutes.

SOURCE: Priscilla F. Leavitt, Ph.D., Parkersburg, WV.

THE GREAT GLOSSARY SEARCH

OBJECTIVE: To utilize the power of advance expectations, peer competition (or teamwork), or social facilitation (improved performance in the presence of others working on similar tasks) to stimulate participants to become familiar with key terms introduced in the training session.

PROCEDURE: Distribute a list of key terms at the beginning of the workshop. Ask participants to listen carefully, read thoroughly, and (if appropriate) collaborate with each other to obtain accurate definitions of the terms prior to the end of the course. (Make sure that it is possible for the definitions to be found!) You may also choose to drop hints where the terms may be located, or you may willingly engage in break-time discussions that help clarify the terms for the more-interested individuals. Be sure to set aside time at the end to provide closure to the exercise.

DISCUSSION QUESTIONS:
1. Which terms were most difficult to identify?
2. What additional sources did you contact to complete the task?
3. How many of you teamed together to define some terms? Did this help?
4. How will this task, featuring independent responsibility and active learning, help you to retain an understanding of these terms in the future?

MATERIALS REQUIRED: Advance list of key terms for the course; follow-up list of appropriately-defined terms to distribute.

APPROXIMATE TIME NEEDED: 5 minutes to explain the task; appropriate time at the end of the workshop to determine whether all participants completed the task accurately or need help from the group or you to finish it.

SOURCE: The authors.

WILL THE REAL MR./MS. JONES STAND UP?

OBJECTIVE: To demonstrate the importance of graphic communication in showing how even simple business cards connote a strong image and message.

PROCEDURE: Individuals are asked to take out their business cards (if some don't have cards, provide them with 3 x 5 index cards). On the back side of the card, ask them to make a picture that describes themselves in any creative way. These can be sketches of themselves, their hobbies, jobs, interests, or family. Anything that can describe themselves is fair game! Collect all the cards in a container. The cards are then drawn at random and the person picking out a card is asked to look at the drawing, not the name side of the card. The introducer then tells the group as much as possible by interpreting the sketch. They can make any assumptions or inferences they so desire. After each "introduction", the person who drew that sketch stands and clarifies, corrects, or more truthfully completes his/her introduction. That person then pulls out another card and proceeds to "introduce" that individual. Continue the process until all persons are introduced.

DISCUSSION QUESTIONS:
1. Why do we stick so closely to "just the facts" in our self-introductions--name, job, and employer?
2. How comfortable did you feel disclosing, through art, other aspects about yourself?
3. What were some of the more interesting things discovered?

MATERIALS REQUIRED: 3 x 5 cards.

APPROXIMATE TIME NEEDED: 15-20 minutes, dependent on group size.

SOURCE: Unknown.

X.

SELF-CONCEPT

I LIKE ME BECAUSE

OBJECTIVE: To allow participants to practice improving their self-esteem in an enjoyable manner.

PROCEDURE: Ask the group members to find a partner--preferably someone that they don't know.
Have them sit in chairs facing their partner.
Ask them to decide who will go first and then tell them to make eye contact with one another, get comfortable, maintain an open body position (don't cross arms, etc.), and speak to their partner about the topic "What do I like about myself?"
Let them talk for 2 minutes. The passive partner cannot say a word, but through body language should express keen interest in the other person.
At the end of 2 minutes, have them switch roles. Then the other partner--again without interruption--must talk for two minutes on "What I like about myself."

DISCUSSION QUESTIONS:

1. What kinds of things do people like about themselves?
2. What kinds of things were noticeably not very frequently mentioned?
3. Why are we reluctant to express a positive self image to others?
4. What are some relatively "safe" ways in which we can express our self-esteem at work?
5. What suggestions do you have for helping to build someone's self-esteem?

MATERIALS REQUIRED: None.

APPROXIMATE TIME NEEDED: 6-8 minutes.

SOURCE: Jack Canfield, Culver City, CA.

I'M OK, I REALLY AM!

OBJECTIVES: To reinforce one's self-esteem and to provide an opportunity to practice empathetic listening.

PROCEDURE: Ask the group to think about three eras of their life-- namely, during their childhood years, when they were in school, and now. Tell them to think about each of these three time frames, and recall something that they did--or that happened to them-- that really made them very proud. (Examples could be "when I was 8th grade spelling champion," or "when I sold 9 homes last month," etc.)

After each person has written down the three things, form groups of 3 people. One person identifies the three proud moments in the three areas, and the person to the first speaker's right listens carefully to the comments and then must interpret not what the person said, but rather, what that person probably meant.

Another person listening makes no verbal comment, but takes a stick-on note and writes out a truthful and sincere compliment to the original speaker and verbally gives praise to the speaker on those accomplishments and attaches the stick-on note to the person's clothing. After the first round, the process is repeated with a second person reporting, another interpreting what the statements meant, and the third participant writing out the compliment on a stick-on note. Repeat for the third person.

DISCUSSION QUESTIONS:
1. How many feel comfortable praising yourselves?
2. How many periodically review past successes?
3. Do you know someone who can/will praise you?
4. How did it feel to have an empathetic listener?

MATERIALS. REQUIRED: Stick-on notepads for each small group.

APPROXIMATE TIME NEEDED: 10-15 minutes.

SOURCE: Sue Pistone, Houston, TX.

MIND OVER BODY

OBJECTIVE: To demonstrate the subtle forces of kinesiology and the nervous system.

PROCEDURE: Ask the group members to stand and find a partner. Tell them you're going to demonstrate how our physical actions frequently reflect our mental state. Decide which person will be partner "A" and "B". Partner "A's" should think back in the past few months to a very positive experience, (i.e., a situation where they really had a peak performance). Ask them to close their eyes and nod to their partner when they have a mental picture of that event. Ask Partner "A's" to raise their right arm parallel with the floor, still with their eyes closed. Ask "B's" to move closer to "A's" and place their left hand on "A's" arm. Ask "A's" to state their name aloud and ask "B's" to try and push "A's" arm downward as "A" resists. (Likely, Partner "A" will be able to withstand that pressure.)
Now ask "B's" to think of a recent experience that was not a pleasant one at all. Ask "B's" to close their eyes and nod when they have that negative thought in mind. Ask them to raise their right arm as "A's" place their left hands on "B's" arm. Tell "B's" to select a fictitious name and say that aloud, i.e., "My name is John Doe" and tell "A's" to push down while "B's" resist. (In most cases, the arm will easily be pushed downward.)

DISCUSSION QUESTIONS:
1. What is the typical impact on our body of being happy and truthful?
2. What is the typical impact on our body of feeling negative? Being untruthful?

MATERIALS REQUIRED: None.

APPROXIMATE TIME NEEDED: 3-5 minutes.

SOURCE: Jack Canfield, Culver City, CA.

MY NOVEL LIFE

OBJECTIVE: To enable participants to identify significant life events and the corresponding impacts on their adult life.

PROCEDURE: Tell the group they will be given a "novel" experience in writing their own "best selling novel". Allow 15-20 minutes for them to write a novel on their life from birth to death featuring two important pieces of information.

First, ask them to recall and write out a list of four or five events that they can think of from their past. Identify the particular events and how they felt about those particular events.

Secondly, ask them to take a peek into the future and predict 3-4 events that will happen to them. Write these out and comment on why they feel these events will indeed occur to them.

When completed, form the participants into dyads and invite them to discuss their novel lives with each other.

DISCUSSION QUESTIONS:
1. How have those earlier events affected your life as an adult?
2. Have these events affected your feelings about yourself or others?
3. How do your future events compare with past events?
4. How do past events differ from your predicted future?

MATERIALS REQUIRED: Blank paper and pencils.

APPROXIMATE TIME NEEDED: 25-30 minutes.

SOURCE: Venus Sage, Ann Arbor, MI.

XI.

SUCCESS

AND

LEADERSHIP

IT'S POKER TIME!

OBJECTIVE: To demonstrate some of the dysfunctional effects of classic managerial efforts to improve productivity.

PROCEDURE: Designate yourself as CEO. Identify five people as workers, and a sixth as their manager. Give each worker a deck of cards (with jokers removed). Indicate that their individual performance will be scored after each of six rounds, based on the number of errors (defined as face cards) that appear in a draw of five cards per person. Have them shuffle their decks and deal out five cards. Ask the manager to record the number of errors per person, record it on the scoring sheet, and report the results to you. Berate the manager verbally, and exhort him/her to counsel those with errors to improve. Conduct a second and third round and repeat the berating process (with no probable improvement). For rounds 4-6, relent and tell the workers that if they draw, or create through trading in a 30-second period, a "pat" poker hand you will find that acceptable despite the presence of face cards. Record the results and lead a discussion.

DISCUSSION QUESTIONS:
1. Will some employees, when pressured, do whatever it takes to make themselves look good?
2. Will some employees cover up for other workers?
3. Are employees ever punished for accurately reporting problems? Rewarded for "good" data?
4. Does upper management always really know what is going on in the organization?

MATERIALS REQUIRED: Five decks of playing cards; score sheet; and an instructional sheet defining "pat hands" in poker-- full house, straight, flush, straight flush, royal flush.

APPROXIMATE TIME NEEDED: 30 minutes, depending on depth of discussion.

SOURCE: Christopher Storey, "Excellence: It's in the Cards," Training and Development Journal, September, 1989, pp. 46-48.

SCORING SHEET

Worker	Round					
	1	2	3	4	5	6
A. _____						
B. _____						
C. _____						
D. _____						
E. _____						
Overall results: ___						

Pat hands:
- Full house: a pair, & 3 of a kind
- Straight: any 5 consecutive cards
- Flush: any 5 cards of one suit
- Straight flush: 5 consecutive cards of one suit
- Royal flush: the ace, king, queen, jack, and ten of one suit

LEADERSHIP PRE-POST TEST

OBJECTIVE: To allow participants to do some self-assessment and to identify areas in need of improvement.

PROCEDURE: Adapt the Leadership Pre-Post Test as needed to fit the particular type of content session being covered. Distribute copies to all participants at the start of the session and ask them to individually assess their leadership (or other) skills as shown.
Do not collect the papers, but ask participants to hold them for later use.
At the conclusion of the program, ask them to bring out their forms and individually answer the same questions.

DISCUSSION QUESTIONS:
1. What was the range of the group's total scores?
2. Which items are of greatest interest to you (the ones you indicated you wanted to learn more about)?
3. How have you acquired knowledge or skill in these areas?
4. What can you do in the future to further extend your knowledge?
5. What topics in this workshop were most useful for adding to your self-assessed capabilities?

MATERIALS REQUIRED: Copies of the Leadership Pre-Post Test.

APPROXIMATE TIME NEEDED: 3-5 minutes at the start of the program; 3-5 minutes at the program's conclusion.

SOURCE: Russ Haag, Brewton, AL.

LEADERSHIP PRE-POST TEST

Name_____

Assess your leadership skills on a scale from 1-10 (where 1 = low and 10 = very high). Mark an "X" on the number below each statement.

_____1) How much do you know about how to motivate people?
        1   2   3   4   5   6   7   8   9   10

_____2) How good are you at talking to groups and communicating?
        1   2   3   4   5   6   7   8   9   10

_____3) How do you think others would rate you as a leader?
        1   2   3   4   5   6   7   8   9   10

_____4) How would you rate yourself as a leader?
        1   2   3   4   5   6   7   8   9   10

_____5) How good are you at dealing with difficult people?
        1   2   3   4   5   6   7   8   9   10

_____6) How likely are you to introduce yourself to people you don't know?
        1   2   3   4   5   6   7   8   9   10

_____7) How much do you know about leadership?
        1   2   3   4   5   6   7   8   9   10

_____8) How much leadership experience do you have?
        1   2   3   4   5   6   7   8   9   10

_____9) How well do you work under pressure?
        1   2   3   4   5   6   7   8   9   10

_____10) How important are you to the overall success of your organization?
        1   2   3   4   5   6   7   8   9   10

_____ TOTAL SCORE (Add your answers together and mark the total.)

NOW READ THE QUESTIONS AGAIN AND CHECK, IN THE LEFT-HAND COLUMN, THE THREE TOPICS THAT YOU WOULD LIKE TO LEARN MORE ABOUT.

SUCCESS IS...

OBJECTIVE: To provide an opportunity for participants to compare and contrast their value systems at various points in their lives.

PROCEDURE: In discussing success, leadership, values, or related topics, ask the group to think about the word "success" and how they perceive it.

First, ask them to think back to the time they were "kids," and individually write out what "success" meant to them, or how they might have "seen" or identified that word at that time. For example, they might--as younger children--have equated "success" with rock stars, movie personalities, sports heroes, etc. Allow 2-3 minutes for this.

Second, ask them to write down how they "saw" or identified success when they were leaving school or graduating from college. (Answers often will measure success in monetary figures, i.e., making $25-100,000 a year.) Give them 2-3 minutes.

Third, ask them to think about "success" today. Ask them to jot down their thoughts or comments as to how they identify success or what does success mean to them. (Responses typically are in terms of job satisfaction, service activities, career or family achievements, etc.) Allow them a few minutes to write out their responses.

Then divide them into groups of 3-4 participants and ask them to compare answers and discuss the similarities or differences in their "definitions".

**DISCUSSION
QUESTIONS:**
1. How did you define success at different periods?
2. Why is there such a change?
3. What have you learned from others' responses?

**MATERIALS
REQUIRED:** Paper and pencils.

**APPROXIMATE
TIME NEEDED:** 15-20 minutes.

SOURCE: Unknown.

TRAITS OF LEADERSHIP

OBJECTIVE: To identify qualities of leadership believed to be useful for success in today's business world.

PROCEDURE: In a discussion of management, leadership, or team-building, ask the group to think of people (in business, government, religion, education, or any endeavor) that they consider to be real "leaders". Ask them to jot down 5 or 6 names of people that seem to "jump" into their mind when they think of "leader". Give them a minute or two to write these names down, and then ask them to make a note or two about each individual as to <u>why</u> they are perceived as a leader.
Divide the participants into groups of 3-4 persons and ask them to compare their lists of names and the contributing qualities.

DISCUSSION QUESTIONS:
1. What are some of the leaders' names that were mentioned?
2. How many thought of _____? (Repeat 3-4 responses from Question 1, to obtain a measure of the frequency of response or overlap.)
3. Why were these names suggested so often?
4. Who wrote down a name that many of us may <u>not</u> know? Why did that person's name come to mind?
5. How do your responses compare with the results of decades of research on leadership traits?
6. Are good leaders born, or can they be "made"?

MATERIALS REQUIRED: Paper and pencils.

APPROXIMATE TIME NEEDED: 10 minutes.

SOURCE: Unknown.

VALUE ADDED

OBJECTIVE: To identify those areas of job responsibilities that may or may not be adding value to the organization.

PROCEDURE: Pose the following questions to the group:
Suppose that you had more time to do the activities that you honestly believe you are better trained, more experienced, etc., to do--activities that you believe would definitely be "Value Added" to your organization, but that right now, you just can't do. What are those activities?
Ask participants to think seriously about the question and write down their responses on a piece of paper. Allow 5 minutes for this, and then the second key question:
Some activities you perform probably don't utilize your talents as much as they could. These activities are not considered "Value Added," but they seem to consume a big portion of your time and energy. These are the kinds of job activities that you have to do, but frankly, you wish you did not have to do so much, or even at all. What are those activities?
Again ask the group to ponder the question, and write out their responses (5 minutes).
Subdivide the total group into triads and ask them to share their individual comments and insights into "Value Added" activities in the next 5-10 minutes.

**DISCUSSION
QUESTIONS:**
1. What are some of the tasks you feel you could be doing to help your organization improve?
2. What can you do about the items in question 1?
3. What are some activities you could forget about?
4. Are there some activities that you could or perhaps should be delegating to others?

**MATERIALS
REQUIRED:**   None.

**APPROXIMATE
TIME NEEDED:** 20-25 minutes.

SOURCE: Frank Helton, Fountain Hills, AZ.

WHERE'S THE FIRE?

OBJECTIVE: To demonstrate the value of prioritizing items of importance.

PROCEDURE: Inform participants that they are about to engage in a mental role-play exercise.
Ask them to assume they are all at their desks or work stations when the fire alarm sounds. Over the public address system, your CEO (or boss) announces that each person is to vacate the premises in one minute! He/she states that each person is allowed to bring with them a maximum of five items from their offices. They must be items that can be carried out with them (i.e., no desks, file cabinets, water coolers). Then ask them to provide a response to the following task:
"In the next 60 seconds, write down those items you have decided to take with you."
NOTE: Allow the participants a minute or so to jot down their list on a blank sheet of paper. After it appears that most people have completed the task, discuss these questions in groups of 3-4 participants.

DISCUSSION QUESTIONS:
1. How easy (or difficult) was it to select five items?
2. Of the items you picked, how many were job-related (i.e., a policy manual), as opposed to those of a personal nature (i.e., a family picture)?
3. How many of you had difficulty even picking 4-5 items to take with you?
4. Why did you pick the items you did?
5. In what domains of your (work) life do you regularly prioritize items? Why or why not?

MATERIALS: REQUIRED: Paper and pencils.

APPROXIMATE TIME NEEDED: 15 minutes.

SOURCE: Dr. Barbara J. Wilkie, Atlanta, GA.

XII.

TEAMBUILDING

AND

GROUPS

ANYTHING I CAN DO, WE CAN DO BETTER

OBJECTIVE: To demonstrate the merits of group decision-making on one kind of a task.

PROCEDURE: Distribute a copy of the form on page 309 to each participant. Instruct them to rank-order the ten items from 1-10 (1=highest; 10=lowest) according to the degree to which workers nationwide considered that reason "very important" in deciding to take their current job. Results should be entered in column 2.
Break the participants into small groups of 3-5 persons and repeat the process, with the ranking numbers placed in column 4.
Display the key on a transparency, have them enter it in column 3 of their sheets, and then compute the absolute arithmetic differences between each of their item rankings and the key (without regard to positive or negative sign). Do this for both the individual and group rankings. Then ask them to add up the totals.

DISCUSSION QUESTIONS:
1. Who performed better, individuals or groups?
2. What factors contribute to group success on tasks such as these?
3. How can groups be used more productively at work to capitalize on their assets?
4. What problems might groups be subject to on tasks such as these?

MATERIALS REQUIRED: One copy of handout for each participant.

APPROXIMATE TIME NEEDED: 30-60 minutes, depending on options used and depth of discussion generated.

SOURCE: Title inspired by Allen R. Solem; data obtained from National Study of the Changing Workforce report summarized in Wall Street Journal, Sept. 3, 1993.

IMPORTANT JOB FACTORS

DIRECTIONS: Rank-order the following items from 1-10 (1=highest; 10=lowest) according to your estimate of the degree to which workers in a nationwide study reported that reason to be "very important" in deciding to take their current job.

	1	2	3	4	5
Advancement opportunity					
Control over work content					
Flexible work schedule					
Fringe benefits					
Job security					
Nature of the work					
Open communication					
Salary/wages					
Size of organization					
Stimulating work					

KEY: IMPORTANT JOB FACTORS

	Rank
Advancement opportunity	8
Control over work content	3
Flexible work schedule	7
Fringe benefits	6
Job security	4
Nature of the work	2
Open communication	1
Salary/wages	9
Size of organization	10
Stimulating work	5

Source: "Work Force Study Finds Loyalty is Weak,"
Wall Street Journal, Sept. 3, 1993, p. B-1.

FAMOUS FEMALES

OBJECTIVES: To provide an opportunity for participants to work together and pool their knowledge; to demonstrate the role of selective perception on learning/recall.

PROCEDURE: Form the participants into small groups of 3-5 persons each. You may wish to purposely construct some groups of all females, some of all males, and others with mixed gender.
Instruct the groups to generate a list of the "Ten Most Important American Women." Be sure they understand that this covers the entire period of our nation's history since European explorers first came to America.
After about 10 minutes, stop the groups and allow them to score themselves with 10 points for every name that matches one on the master list. Then lead a discussion focused on the following questions.
Alternative: Provide them with a list of the 25 names, and ask them to correctly identify <u>why</u> each person might appear on that list.

DISCUSSION QUESTIONS:
1. How well did you do?
2. Why were some groups (or individuals) more successful than others?
3. What does this exercise tell us about education, socialization, learning, and retention?
4. How does selective perception influence people at work? In this workshop?

MATERIALS REQUIRED: Transparency (or handouts) of the list on page 315.

APPROXIMATE TIME NEEDED: 20-30 minutes.

SOURCE: <u>Ladies' Home Journal</u>, in consultation with the Institute for Research in History and the Schlesinger Library at Radcliffe College.

IMPORTANT AMERICAN WOMEN

1. Martha Washington, first U.S. "first lady."
2. Sacajawea, Indian guide for Lewis and Clark.
3. Lydia Pinkham, seller of patent medicines.
4. Harriet Beecher Stowe, Uncle Tom's Cabin author.
5. Susan B. Anthony, feminist.
6. Harriet Tubman, helper of escaping slaves.
7. Mary Baker Eddy, founder of Christian Science.
8. Clara Barton, founder of American Red Cross.
9. Louisa May Alcott, author of Little Women.
10. Frances Willard, WCTU leader.
11. Jane Addams, Hull House founder & Nobelist.
12. Isadora Duncan, dancer.
13. Mary Pickford, actress.
14. Margaret Sanger, Planned Parenthood founder.
15. Frances Perkins, first woman in Cabinet (Labor).
16. Eleanor Roosevelt, first lady & humanitarian.
17. Pearl S. Buck, The Good Earth author & Nobelist.
18. Amelia Earhart, trans-Atlantic solo pilot.
19. Clare Boothe Luce, writer, Congresswoman, & ambassador.
20. Rachel Carson, author of Silent Spring.
21. Rosa Parks, catalyst for bus strike against segregation in Montgomery, Alabama.
22. Betty Friedan, author of The Feminine Mystique.
23. Joan Cooley, Children's TV Workshop founder.
24. Sally Ride, first woman astronaut.
25. Geraldine Ferraro, Congresswoman and first female Vice-Presidential candidate.

Source: Ladies' Home Journal.

JIGSAW TEAM-BUILDING

OBJECTIVE: To stress the importance of each team member's individual contributions, and the importance of working as a group.

PROCEDURE: Select a solvable picture puzzle. Break it into sub-sets of 10 connectable pieces each. Distribute a sub-set to each participant (such that the sub-sets could then be connected to each other).
Instruct them to solve their own sub-set first, and then connect all the sub-sets appropriately until they have the total puzzle solved. Set a challenging time limit for the task completion, and possibly play some energizing music (e.g., the William Tell overture, or Wagner's "Ride of the Valkyries") to create an additional sense of urgency.
You may choose to designate a small number of participants as free-floating "trouble-shooters" who roam about the room and help those in trouble to see viable connections within their own sub-set and from one set to another.

DISCUSSION QUESTIONS:
1. What reactions did you have when you realized your importance to the overall team?
2. What impact did the time deadline have on your effectiveness? What impact did the music have on your actions?
3. What was the impact of having team members available (and willing) to help you?

MATERIALS REQUIRED: One previously-constructed picture puzzle, divided into sets of approximately 10 pieces per participant, and then broken apart and allocated to each participant for re-assembly.

APPROXIMATE TIME NEEDED: 15-20 minutes, plus discussion.

SOURCE: David Butler, WordPerfect Pacific, Australia.

SO MUCH IN COMMON

OBJECTIVE: For use in diversity training, to demonstrate that people often have more in common than NOT in common.

PROCEDURE: Distribute copies of the "Commonality Exercise" to each participant. Ask the group members to find a partner quickly. When given the signal to begin, instruct them to find out as many things as they possibly can that the two of them have in common. Ask them to write down their partner's name and jot down, in the first column, the items that they found to be in common.
At the end of 2-3 minutes, call time and ask participants to find a new partner, and at your signal, repeat the process.
Call time after 2-3 minutes and repeat the procedure one more time with new partners.

DISCUSSION QUESTIONS:
1. How many of you found more than 15 things in common?
2. What were some of the unusual items you discovered?
3. How did you uncover these areas of commonality?
4. Is it likely that in most situations, we may well find similar results, i.e., we have much more in common than we otherwise might think?
5. What implications does this have for us as members of a diverse work force?

MATERIALS REQUIRED: Copies of "Commonality Exercise" form.

APPROXIMATE TIME NEEDED: 8-10 minutes.

SOURCE: Lenora Billings-Harris, Chandler, AZ.

COMMONALITY EXERCISE

List the things you find in common with three other people in the workshop.

NAME_____

1_____
2_____
3_____
4_____
5_____
6_____
7_____
8_____
9_____
10_____
11_____
12_____
13_____
14_____
15_____

NAME_____

1_____
2_____
3_____
4_____
5_____
6_____
7_____
8_____
9_____
10_____
11_____
12_____
13_____
14_____
15_____

NAME_____

1_____
2_____
3_____
4_____
5_____
6_____
7_____
8_____
9_____
10_____
11_____
12_____
13_____
14_____
15_____

THE JIGSAW PUZZLE

OBJECTIVE: To stimulate participants to acquire and use a simple metaphor or paradigm for the characteristics of effective teams and organizations.

PROCEDURE: Show, or distribute a handout of, the pieces of a jigsaw puzzle to the group. Ask them to list all the ways in which the jigsaw is similar to the composition and operation of a high-performance organization.
Some of the many possibilities include:
1. There are boundaries (the straight-edged pieces).
2. Each piece plays a specific role in the solution.
3. Pieces are highly interconnected.
4. Each piece is unique in its nature (similar to the individual differences among people).
5. The solution is a fragile one (easily broken).
6. The whole is more than the sum of its parts.
7. Some pieces are central, some are peripheral.
8. There are "natural" groupings (e.g., by color).
9. Pieces need someone to move them.
10. Rapid solution is aided by someone with an overall vision of the product.

DISCUSSION QUESTIONS:
1. Are you surprised by the number of similarities?
2. What are the ways in which you can use this metaphor?
3. What action guidelines does this point toward?

MATERIALS REQUIRED: Transparency of jigsaw puzzle pieces.

APPROXIMATE TIME NEEDED: 10 minutes.

SOURCE: Frank Shipper.

JIGSAW PIECES

THE JOY OF SIX

OBJECTIVE: To provide a vivid demonstration of the satisfaction (joy) of being included in a group (of six), and the uneasiness of being excluded.

PROCEDURE: Prepare a series of short messages (e.g., "Things go better with Coke") and make six copies of each. Ideally, the messages relate either to the central topics of the workshop/meeting, or else to currently-important themes or issues in the organization, such as "Total Quality Management."
Make single copies of 1-5 other messages. Place all of these in individual (unmarked) envelopes, seal them, and mix them up.
Instruct participants to open their envelopes, read the message, circulate around the room, introduce themselves, and repeat the message (softly). Tell them to continue this search and introductory process, staying in growing clusters, until they are all experiencing the "joy of six". When all but the "loners" are in their groups of six, act surprised and lead them in the following discussion.

DISCUSSION QUESTIONS:
1. How does it feel to not be accepted into a group? Does this ever happen at work? Is it intentional?
2. How did it feel when you found someone with the same message?
3. Why didn't those persons already in a group reach out to the excluded persons? How do organizational policies, or our own self-interests, prevent us from including others?
4. What can we do to include others "in the loop"?
5. What lessons does this have for team building?

MATERIALS REQUIRED: Sufficient messages and envelopes, prepared in advance, to accommodate all session participants.

APPROXIMATE TIME NEEDED: 10 minutes.

SOURCE: Bill J. Ohlemeier, Association Services for Kansas Electric Cooperatives, Inc., Topeka, Kansas.

TOXIC WASTE DUMP

OBJECTIVES: To provide an opportunity for planning and experiencing teamwork, and a live forum for analyzing its prerequisites, processes, and consequences.

PROCEDURE: Briefly explain to the group how important teams and teamwork are in contemporary organizations. Ask them to identify the characteristics of highly-effective teams. Explain that effective teams pay close attention to both their task and their process (e.g., how they work together to accomplish their objective). Form participants into groups of 6-8 people. Establish an open space for each group, with a 10-foot diameter circle marked off with string. Distribute the instruction sheet on page 331 to each person, and start the clock running. Administer the rules very closely.

DISCUSSION QUESTIONS:
1. Was your team successful? By what measures?
2. What did your team do that helped it succeed?
3. What did your team members do that caused it to have difficulties?
4. What did you learn from this exercise that you can apply on the job?

MATERIALS REQUIRED: Two coffee cans, enough popcorn kernels to fill one can about halfway, 6-8 pieces of 7 1/2-foot-long rope, and one bicycle tire tube. Suggestion: select a green can for the "safe" one; a red can for the toxic one.

APPROXIMATE TIME NEEDED: 60 minutes.

SOURCE: Pam Lindberg (and Keith Merron), Ann Arbor, MI.

TOXIC WASTE DUMP: INSTRUCTIONS

BACKGROUND: A can of highly toxic popcorn has contaminated a circle approximately 10 feet in diameter. The toxic area extends to the ceiling. If the poisonous popcorn is not transferred to a safe container for decontamination, the toxic popcorn will contaminate and destroy the population of the entire city. The popcorn is estimated to have a safe life of exactly 30 minutes before it explodes. Obviously, there is insufficient time to contact authorities and evacuate the city. Therefore, the lives of thousands of people are in your hands.

Inside the circle you will find two cans. One (unsafe) container is about half full of the toxic popcorn. The other (safe) container is available for decontamination.

OBJECTIVE: You must find a way to safely transfer the toxic popcorn from the unsafe container to the safe container, using only the materials provided to you. For your group, this includes a piece of rope (each approximately 7 1/2 feet long) for each person, and a bicycle tire tube.

RULES:
1. NO participant may cross the plane of the circle with any part of the body. If this occurs, they must be taken to the hospital immediately (removed from play) and they may not participate in any form from then on. The group is responsible for the safety of all its members.

2. NO participant may sacrifice him/herself to aid in the transfer of popcorn.

3. NO spills are allowed, or the popcorn will explode.

4. Participants may ONLY use the materials provided. However, they can be used in any way desired.

5. The popcorn will not spread its toxicity to the safe can, the ropes, the tube, or the instruction-giver. The participants have no protection inside the imaginary cylinder created by the 10-foot diameter rope.

6. The safe container may move anywhere in or outside of the circle. The unsafe container must stay inside the circle, and not be moved more than one foot from its center.

7. Remember, the popcorn must be transferred within 30 minutes, or there will be a tremendous disaster.

WE NEED YOU!

OBJECTIVES: To demonstrate that every single person is an important part of any group or organization.

PROCEDURE: Collect several full page (at least 8" x 11") color ads from magazines and make a black and white copy of each. Keep the copied ads intact, and cut the original color ads into six parts--much like a puzzle. On the back of each part of each picture, write the picture number (i.e., on the back of all six parts of picture #1, write "1"). Do the same for picture #2, and so on. Take one piece from each picture and keep it. Mix up the rest of the pieces and give one to each participant. Ask them to find the other people with pieces they need to make a complete picture. After a few minutes, display the black and white copy of each picture so they know what they're looking for. Tell them that six pieces make a full picture. If, after 5-7 minutes, some groups are still struggling, tell them all about the numbers on the back. Even with this information, however, they will still have some problems, for the missing piece that you have prevents them from solving the task.

DISCUSSION QUESTIONS:
1. What happens when a key element is missing?
2. What happens when a group member is missing?
3. How did you feel when you learned about the numbers on the back?
4. How did you feel when you knew you were not given all the information (i.e., not being told about the missing piece)?
5. Have you encountered situations when you didn't have all of the information you needed? What did you do?

MATERIALS REQUIRED: Several full page color ads from magazines.

APPROXIMATE TIME NEEDED: 15-20 minutes depending on size of group.

SOURCE: Dr. Susan Shoemaker, Phoenix, AZ.

HELP WANTED!

We invite you to become a contributor to future books of "Games Trainers Play." If you have developed an original activity that might be shared with your colleagues in the profession, we'd appreciate hearing from you. You can use this form (make copies if needed) and send it in. If you know of the source or originator, that's very important to include for proper credit. Thank You!

TITLE: _____

OBJECTIVE(S): _____

_____

_____

PROCEDURE: _____

_____

_____

_____

_____

_____

**MATERIALS
REQUIRED:** _____

**APPROXIMATE
TIME NEEDED:** _____

SOURCE: _____

PLEASE RETURN TO EITHER:

Edward E. Scannell
4234 N. Winfield Scott Plaza
Suite 101
Scottsdale, AZ 85251
(602-970-0101)

Dr. John W. Newstrom
Univ. of Minnesota, Duluth
SBE 110
Duluth, MN 55812
(218-726-8762)